THE COMPLETE
COOKIE BOOK

THE COMPLETE COOKIE BOOK

CREATIVE AND DELICIOUS IDEAS FOR MAKING AND DECORATING COOKIES

ELIZABETH WOLF COHEN

CHARTWELL
BOOKS, INC.

Published in 2003 by Chartwell Books
A Division of Book Sales, Inc.
114 Northfield Avenue
Edison, New Jersey 08837

This edition produced for sale in the U.S.A., its
territories, and dependencies only.

A QUINTET BOOK

Reprinted 1996, 1997, 2003

ISBN 0-7858-1732-8

This book was designed and produced by
Quintet Publishing Limited
6 Blundell Street
London N7 9BH

Designer: Ian Hunt
Project Editor: Anna Briffa
Photographer: Nick Bailey

Creative Director: Richard Dewing
Publisher: Oliver Salzmann

Typeset in Great Britain by
Central Southern Typesetters, Eastbourne
Manufactured in Singapore by
Eray Scan (Pte) Ltd.
Printed in Singapore by
Star Standard Industries (Pte) Ltd.

CONTENTS

INTRODUCTION

The first thing I can remember baking was a batch of chocolate chip cookies, made by following the recipe on the back of the package of chocolate chips. They were a great success with my three younger brothers, although they were probably not that critical, and I have been baking ever since. Although I have graduated to more sophisticated and complicated efforts, chocolate chip cookies have become a standard item in my repertoire.

Cookies were first introduced to colonial America by the New York Dutch, who brought their *Koekjes* or "little cakes" from their homeland. Until wood-burning or coal-fired ovens were in general use, cookie baking would have been unreliable at best. By the early 20th century, cookies were so popular that special jars and tins were produced. Since then, there has been no looking back – in the last 10 to 15 years cookies have become so popular that there are now special stores selling fresh baked cookies from every street corner!

Every nation seems to have a special cookie – chocolate chip cookies and brownies from America, tea biscuits like Shrewsbury biscuits from England, shortbread from Scotland, tuiles from France, gingerbread from Sweden, Germany and other northern European countries – the list is endless.

Cookies are one of life's great treats. Even the strictest of dieters and those who deny having a sweet tooth will splurge and have a cookie with a glass of milk or a cup of tea or coffee. And the bonus is they are almost always easy to make.

The six basic types of cookie are generally determined by the way the dough is shaped.

DROP COOKIES are usually dropped or pushed from a spoon directly onto a baking sheet, leaving about a 2-inch space between each to allow for spreading.

MOLDED COOKIES are usually shaped with the hands into balls, logs or cylinders before placing on baking sheets; some molded cookies are actually baked in molds. Molded cookies do not usually spread, so less space is required between them.

REFRIGERATOR COOKIES are made from a rich, stiff, pastry-like dough, rolled into log shapes and then sliced as required for baking. Most of these doughs can be refrigerated for several days or frozen for up to 6 months. The advantage with refrigerator cookies is that they can be sliced and baked almost on demand.

ROLLED COOKIES are made from a dough which is rolled out with a rolling pin, then cut into shapes using a knife or cookie cutters. These are popular with children as cutters are now available in so many fun shapes. These cookies are often decorated with colored icings.

PRESSED COOKIES are formed by pressing the dough through a cookie press or pastry bag and nozzle onto the baking sheet.

BAR COOKIES are formed by spreading a soft dough in a shallow pan, with or without a topping, then baking. After cooling they are cut into bars, squares, diamonds or triangles.

SPECIAL COOKIES are usually shaped by one of the above methods, and then either formed into tuiles or tulips, or fried or baked in a waffle iron, to achieve a special effect.

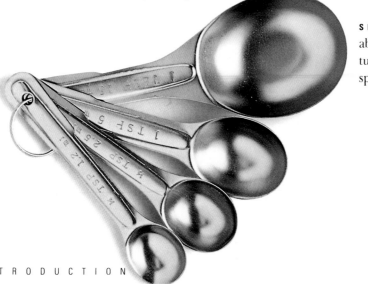

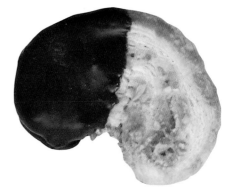

TIPS FOR SUCCESSFUL COOKIE BAKING

Cookie making is generally easy and requires very little equipment, but always be sure to read the recipe through before you begin. Always assemble the ingredients together before you start to cook, then put them aside or return them to their storage places as you use them, that way you'll never forget an ingredient or include it twice.

EQUIPMENT AND PANS

Almost all cookie doughs can be made by hand (they all started that way) or with an electric mixer or in a food processor. I suggest an electric mixer, as it gives the baker more of a feel and control over the dough. Use heavy-gauge, flat, shiny aluminum baking sheets. They should be at least 2 inches smaller than the inside of your oven, so that the heat can circulate evenly. (Dark ones may cause overbrowning.) Non-stick pans are ideal for certain cookies, but may cause others to spread too much (this will be indicated in specific recipes). New "Cushionaire" baking sheets are excellent, especially for thin cookies or meringues, which tend to overbrown on the bottom. It is like baking on double baking sheets, but not so cumbersome.

Grease cookie sheets only when indicated, otherwise cookies may spread too much or become too thin. Most butter-rich cookie doughs don't require greased baking sheets, but a very thin layer of butter can be used as a precaution. I like to use a "baking spray" for the lightest of coatings, or I use a pastry brush to ensure an even coating.

Evenly space cookies on baking sheets, and do not leave any large gaps. Arrange 2 baking sheets in the lower and upper thirds of the oven; a single baking sheet should always be placed in the center of the oven. Rotate the baking sheets from the bottom shelf to the top and from back to front, halfway through cooking time. If you do not have enough baking sheets, arrange the cookies on sheets of heavy-duty foil, or baking parchment, cut to fit baking sheets. As soon as baked cookies are removed from the oven, slide them off onto a rack, then slide a sheet of foil with the next batch of cookies onto baking sheet and continue to bake immediately. *Never put cookies directly onto a hot baking sheet.* For quick cooling, run back of baking sheet under cold running water and wipe dry; then regrease if necessary.

MIXING AND BAKING

As with all baking, measure the ingredients carefully. I use unsalted butter, as it generally contains less water and impurities, and large eggs. All the recipes have been tested with all-purpose flour although in some recipes cake flour is just as suitable; it is not essential to sift the flour, but it facilitates the mixing up of the dry ingredients and insures any lumps are eliminated. Always soften the butter and cream well with the sugar, but mix in flour and dry ingredients gently or the dough may toughen.

Preheat the oven to the required temperature (if you are in doubt, double check with an oven thermometer). Use a kitchen timer and check for doneness several minutes before the end of the suggested baking time. Do not overbake cookies or they may be too dry and taste stale. Because they are thin, they continue to bake even when removed from the oven. As soon as they are firm enough, remove cookies to wire racks to cool in a single layer.

STORING AND FREEZING

Most cookies can be stored in airtight containers or cookie jars or tins. Store different kinds of cookies separately, as the flavors might blend or moist cookies might soften crisp cookies. Delicate or sticky cookies should be separated by sheets of waxed paper or foil. To recrisp cookies, reheat for 3 to 5 minutes on a baking sheet in a 300°F oven.

Most cookie doughs can be stored in the refrigerator for several days or wrapped tightly in plastic wrap or freezer bags, then frozen. To use frozen dough, thaw, still wrapped, at room temperature until soft enough to handle, then shape or slice and bake. Refrigerator cookie dough should be thawed in the refrigerator until just soft enough to slice.

Although I prefer cookies to be freshly baked, most baked cookies freeze well and are quick to thaw on short notice. Freeze in small quantities in heavy-duty freezer bags or small airtight containers, expelling as much air as possible.

1

DROP
Cookies

The cookie mixture is pushed

straight from the spoon onto the baking sheet.

Remember to allow room for spreading.

LEBKUCHEN

LEFT & BELOW

ABOUT 3 DOZEN

This famous spiced honey cookie is a traditional Austrian Christmas cookie. It has a cakey texture, flavored with honey and lots of spices. Because they contain no fat, they keep for months.

INGREDIENTS

◊ 2 cups all-purpose flour

◊ ½ cup rye flour

◊ 2 tsp baking powder

◊ 1½ tsp ground cinnamon

◊ 1 tsp ground nutmeg

◊ 1 tsp ground cloves

◊ 1 tsp ground allspice

◊ ½ tsp finely ground black pepper

◊ ½ tsp salt

◊ 1 egg, lightly beaten

◊ 1 cup honey

◊ ¾ cup packed light or dark brown sugar

◊ grated zest of 1 lemon

◊ 1 tbsp fresh lemon juice

◊ 1 cup chopped almonds or walnuts

◊ 1 cup diced candied citron (lemon peel)

GLAZE

◊ 1½ cups confectioners' sugar, sifted

◊ 4 tsp lemon juice

◊ 3 tsp water

◊ Preheat oven to 350°F. Lightly grease 2 large baking sheets. Into a large bowl, sift together flours, baking powder, cinnamon, nutmeg, cloves, allspice, pepper and salt. Remove 1 cup of flour mixture and set aside. Make a well in center of remaining mixture, and add egg, honey, sugar, lemon zest and juice.

◊ With electric mixer at low speed, and beginning in the well, beat ingredients until blended. Add nuts, candied citron and reserved flour to form a stiff dough.

◊ Drop heaped tablespoonfuls, 2 inches apart, onto prepared baking sheets. Bake 20 minutes or until cake tester or toothpick inserted in center comes out clean. Remove cookies to wire rack to cool. Repeat with remaining cookie dough.

◊ In a small bowl, mix confectioners' sugar, lemon juice and water to form glaze. Arrange cookies on wire rack over baking sheet (to catch drips), and pour a little glaze over each cookie to cover tops. (The glaze will crack as it dries.) Store cookies in airtight containers.

OLD-FASHIONED VANILLA WAFERS

NOT ILLUSTRATED

ABOUT 4 DOZEN

These light but luscious wafers resemble a commercial vanilla wafer from my childhood, but I think these are even better.

INGREDIENTS

◊ 1⅓ cups all-purpose flour
◊ ¾ tsp baking powder
◊ ¼ tsp salt
◊ ½ cup (1 stick) unsalted butter, softened
◊ 1 cup superfine sugar
◊ 1 tsp vanilla extract
◊ 1 egg, lightly beaten

◊ Preheat oven to 350°F. Into a medium bowl, sift together flour, baking powder and salt. In another bowl, beat butter until creamy, 1 to 2 minutes. Add sugar and beat 2 minutes, until light and fluffy. Beat in vanilla extract and egg. Stir in flour mixture until well-blended.

◊ Drop half-tablespoonfuls, 2 to 3 inches apart, onto 2 large ungreased baking sheets. Bake 10 to 12 minutes, until cookies are golden-brown around the edges but still pale on top, rotating baking sheets from top to bottom shelf and front to back halfway through cooking time. Remove baking sheets to wire racks to cool slightly. While still warm, using a metal pancake turner or palette knife, carefully remove cookies to wire racks to cool completely. Repeat with remaining cookie mixture.

◊ These cookies are crisp and fragile, but can be stored in airtight containers with waxed paper between the layers.

FRUITY OATMEAL COOKIES

OPPOSITE, ABOVE & RIGHT

ABOUT 3 DOZEN

For a chewy texture be sure to use old-fashioned rolled oats or quick cooking oatmeal, as oat groats will not have enough moisture to soften sufficiently.

INGREDIENTS

◊ 3 cups raisins
◊ 1 cup golden raisins
◊ 1 cup boiling water
◊ ¾ cup (1½ sticks) unsalted butter, softened
◊ 1½ cups packed light brown sugar
◊ 2 eggs, lightly beaten
◊ 1½ tsp vanilla extract
◊ 2½ cups all-purpose flour
◊ ½ tsp baking powder
◊ 1½ tsp baking soda
◊ 1 tsp salt
◊ 2 tsp ground cinnamon
◊ 1 tsp ground ginger
◊ ½ tsp ground cloves
◊ 2 cups old-fashioned (rolled) oats
◊ 2 cups chopped walnuts or pecans, lightly toasted
◊ 1½ cups pitted prunes, chopped
◊ 1 cup chopped pitted dates

◊ In a medium bowl, combine raisins and golden raisins. Pour over the boiling water and allow to stand, covered, until plumped, 30 minutes. Drain, reserving ⅓ cup soaking liquid; set aside.

◊ Preheat oven to 400°F. Lightly grease 2 large baking sheets. In a large bowl with electric mixer, beat butter until creamy, about 30 seconds. Add sugar and continue beating until light and fluffy, about 2 minutes; slowly beat in eggs and vanilla extract.

◊ In a medium bowl, sift together flour, baking powder, baking soda, salt, cinnamon, ginger and cloves. Add butter mixture alternately with reserved soaking liquid, mixing well until blended; stir in oats, walnuts or pecans, prunes, dates and soaked raisins.

◊ Drop heaped tablespoonfuls onto baking sheets, at least 3 inches apart. Bake 6 to 8 minutes, until golden and set. Remove baking sheets to wire racks to cool, about 2 minutes. Then remove cookies to wire racks to cool completely. Repeat with remaining cookie dough. Store in airtight container.

CHOCOLATE CHUNK BANANA COOKIES

L E F T & B E L O W

A B O U T 1 5

This is an ideal way to use ripe bananas – they should be very ripe. These cookies are almost like mini cakes, they are so thick.

INGREDIENTS

◊ 1½ cups all-purpose flour

◊ ½ cup wholewheat flour

◊ ¼ cup unsweetened cocoa powder, preferably Dutch-process

◊ 2 tsp baking powder

◊ ¼ tsp baking soda

◊ 1 tsp ground cinnamon

◊ ½ tsp salt

◊ 6 oz semisweet chocolate, chopped

◊ ¾ cup (1½ sticks) unsalted butter, softened

◊ ½ cup sugar

◊ ½ cup light brown sugar

◊ 1 cup mashed bananas (about 2 large ripe bananas)

◊ 1 tsp vanilla extract

◊ 2 eggs, lightly beaten

◊ 1 cup semisweet chocolate chips

◊ 6 oz fine-quality white chocolate, chopped into ¼-inch pieces

◊ 1 cup coarsely chopped walnuts

◊ 1 cup golden raisins

◊ Line 4 large baking sheets with foil, shiny side up. Into a large bowl, sift together flours, cocoa powder, baking powder, baking soda, cinnamon and salt. In a heat-proof bowl placed over a saucepan of simmering water, melt chocolate, stirring frequently, until smooth. Remove from heat to cool slightly.

◊ In a large bowl, with electric mixer, beat butter until creamy, about 30 seconds. Add sugars, mashed bananas and vanilla extract, beat until well blended. Gradually beat in cooled melted chocolate, and continue beating until mixture lightens in color, 1 to 2 minutes. Add eggs and beat until just blended.

◊ Stir in flour mixture until just blended, then stir in chocolate chips, white chocolate, walnuts and golden raisins until well-mixed. Using an ice-cream scoop or ¼-cup measure, scoop up cookie dough, flatten bottom against side of bowl and drop, 3 inches apart, onto foil-lined sheets. Moisten bottom of a drinking glass and flatten each mound slightly. You will only get 5 to 6 cookies on a sheet. Refrigerate 20 minutes.

◊ Preheat oven to 375°F. Bake cookies 2 sheets at a time, 15 to 20 minutes, rotating baking sheets from top to bottom shelf and front to back halfway through cooking time; do not overbake. Cookies are done when top feels slightly firm to the touch. Remove baking sheets to wire racks to cool, 2 minutes. Using a wide metal pancake turner or palette knife, remove each cookie to wire racks to cool completely. Repeat with remaining prepared sheets; remove refrigerated sheets 10 minutes before baking or dough will be too cold. Store in airtight containers with waxed paper between the layers.

> ### TIP
> *I*f possible, bake cookies on double baking sheets to prevent bottom of cookies burning or cooking before tops are cooked. If you have only 2 large baking sheets, shape mixture onto sheets of foil on work surface. When baking sheets are free, cool, then slide on another sheet of the foil with cookies and bake as above.

CHOCOLATE-HAZELNUT DIVINITY

ABOUT 2 DOZEN

Although these meringues may not be technically "cookies," they are always in the box of Christmas cookies baked by my mother's friend, Charlotte, a superb baker.

INGREDIENTS

◊ 4 egg whites, at room temperature

◊ ¼ tsp cream of tartar

◊ 1 cup superfine sugar

◊ 1 tsp cornstarch

◊ 2 tsp vanilla extract

◊ 1 cup hazelnuts, toasted and coarsely chopped

◊ 1 cup semisweet chocolate chips

◊ Preheat oven to 225°F. Line 2 large baking sheets with foil, shiny side up.

◊ In a large bowl with electric mixer, beat egg whites on low speed until foamy. Add cream of tartar, increase speed to medium-high, and continue beating until whites are stiff. Combine 2 tablespoons sugar with cornstarch; set aside. Add remaining sugar to egg whites a tablespoon at a time, beating well after each addition, until sugar is completely dissolved and whites are stiff and glossy, 15 to 20 minutes. Fold in reserved sugar-cornstarch mixture; then fold in vanilla extract, nuts and chocolate chips.

◊ Using a tablespoon, scoop up a mound of meringue; then use another tablespoon to scrape mound off onto baking sheet. Make each meringue with tall rough peaks to form a large spectacular shape.

◊ Bake meringues 2 hours, rotating baking sheets from top to bottom shelf and front to back halfway through cooking time. Turn off heat, but do not open oven for 1 hour. Meringues should be completely dry, but not colored. Remove baking sheets from oven, and peel meringues off foil. Store in airtight containers in single layers to avoid breaking any sharp peaks.

CHEWY HAZELNUT-LEMON BITES

ABOUT 16

These meringue-like cookies are crisp on the outside but nutty and chewy on the inside.

INGREDIENTS

◊ 4 egg whites, at room temperature

◊ ¾ cup superfine sugar

◊ 2 cups chopped hazelnuts

◊ ⅔ cup diced candied citron (lemon peel)

◊ candied citron to decorate

◊ Preheat oven to 250°F. Line a large baking sheet with rice paper. Place egg whites and sugar in top of a double boiler, or a heat-proof bowl over a saucepan of simmering water.

◊ With a hand-held electric mixer, beat whites until stiff and glossy, 4 to 6 minutes. Remove top of double boiler or bowl from water, and continue beating until meringue mixture is completely cold. Fold in chopped nuts and diced citron.

◊ Using a teaspoon, scoop up balls of meringue and push them off with another teaspoon onto the baking sheet, 2 inches apart. Press a piece of candied citron onto top of each mound. Bake until meringue is set, but pale, 12 to 15 minutes; cookies should remain white. Remove baking sheets to wire rack to cool then slide paper with cookies onto rack to cool completely. When cool, gently peel off cookies from paper. Store in airtight containers.

> **TIP**
> Rice paper is an edible paper available in cookware and specialty shops. If you cannot find it, use non-stick baking parchment, brushed very lightly with a flavorless vegetable oil.

PEANUT BUTTER, WHITE CHOCOLATE AND PEANUT COOKIES

ABOUT 18

These luscious cookies should always be made with a commercially prepared peanut butter, as freshly ground or homemade peanut butters may not react the same way in the recipe.

INGREDIENTS

◊ 1 cup freshly shelled peanuts

◊ 1 cup all-purpose flour

◊ ½ tsp baking soda

◊ ¼ tsp salt

◊ ½ cup chunky peanut butter

◊ ½ cup (1 stick) unsalted butter, softened

◊ ½ cup packed light brown sugar

◊ 2 tbsp sugar

◊ 1 egg

◊ 1 tsp vanilla extract

◊ 6 oz fine-quality white chocolate, coarsely chopped

◊ 2 oz semisweet chocolate, melted

◊ In a medium skillet over medium-low heat, toast peanuts until golden and fragrant, about 5 minutes, stirring frequently. Turn onto a plate, and allow to cool.

◊ Preheat oven to 375°F. Into a medium bowl, sift together flour, baking soda and salt. In a large bowl with an electric mixer, beat peanut butter, butter and sugars together until light and fluffy, about 2 to 3 minutes. Add egg and continue beating 2 minutes more; beat in vanilla extract. Stir in flour mixture until well-blended; then stir in white chocolate and toasted peanuts.

◊ Drop heaped tablespoonfuls at least 2 inches apart on 2 large baking sheets, and flatten slightly with back of a moistened spoon. Bake until golden-brown, about 12 to 15 minutes; do not overbake or cookies will be dry. Remove baking sheets to wire racks to cool, 3 to 5 minutes. Then, using a metal pancake turner or palette knife, remove cookies to wire racks to cool completely.

◊ Spoon melted semisweet chocolate into a paper cone (see below). Drizzle over cookies in zig-zag pattern. Allow to set; store cookies in airtight containers.

> **TIP**
> To prepare a paper cone, fold a square of waxed paper in half to form a triangle. With apex of triangle facing you, fold left corner down to center. Fold right corner down, and wrap around folded left corner, forming a cone. Fold ends into cone. Fill cone with chocolate or other liquid, then fold top edges over to enclose filling. Snip off tip to make a hole about ⅛ inch in diameter, or whatever size is required.

WHITE CHOCOLATE, CREAM CHEESE – MACADAMIA DROPS

LEFT & BELOW

ABOUT **4** DOZEN

The combination of white chocolate and macadamia nuts is luscious. Although macadamias are expensive, they are worth it for these cookies.

INGREDIENTS

◊ ½ cup (1 stick) unsalted butter, softened

◊ 8 oz cream cheese, softened

◊ ¾ cup packed light brown sugar

◊ grated zest of 1 lemon

◊ 1½ tsp vanilla extract

◊ 1½ cups all-purpose flour

◊ 2 tsp baking powder

◊ 1 cup coarsely chopped macadamia nuts

◊ 4 oz fine-quality white chocolate, coarsely chopped

◊ confectioners' sugar for dusting

◊ In a large bowl with electric mixer, beat butter and cream cheese until creamy, 1 to 2 minutes, scraping bowl occasionally. Add sugar and continue beating until light and fluffy, 1 to 2 minutes. Beat in lemon zest and vanilla extract.

◊ Into a medium bowl, sift together flour and baking powder, and stir into cream cheese mixture. Stir in chopped nuts and chocolate. Chill dough until firm, 1 to 2 hours.

◊ Preheat oven to 400°F. Lightly grease 2 large baking sheets. Drop heaped teaspoonfuls of mixture 2 inches apart onto baking sheets, and flatten slightly. Bake until puffed and golden, 8 to 10 minutes. Remove baking sheets to wire racks to cool, 5 to 8 minutes. Then, using a metal pancake turner or palette knife, remove cookies to wire racks to cool completely. Repeat with remaining mixture.

◊ When cookies are cool, arrange side by side on wire racks, and dust lightly with confectioners' sugar. Store in airtight containers.

> **TIP**
> *I*f macadamias are salted, rinse briefly under running water; pat dry with paper towels.

CHOCOLATE TURTLES

A B O V E & R I G H T

2 DOZEN

This is a classic old-time favorite, enriched with chocolate and nuts. The pecans are meant to resemble the head, arms and legs of the turtle.

INGREDIENTS

◊ 12 oz semisweet chocolate, chopped

◊ 4 oz (4 squares) unsweetened chocolate, chopped

◊ ¼ cup (½ stick) unsalted butter, cut into pieces

◊ 1½ cups sugar

◊ 4 eggs, lightly beaten

◊ 1 tsp vanilla extract

◊ ½ cup all-purpose flour

◊ 1 tbsp instant espresso powder

◊ ½ tsp baking powder

◊ ¼ tsp salt

◊ 2 cups coarsely chopped pecans or walnuts

◊ 2 cups semisweet chocolate chips

◊ 2 cups pecan halves to decorate

> **TIP**
> *U*nsweetened chocolate is also called bakers' chocolate. It gives an intense chocolate flavor to all baked goods.

◊ Preheat oven to 350°F. Line 2 large baking sheets with foil or non-stick baking parchment. In a medium saucepan over medium-low heat, melt chocolates with butter until smooth, stirring frequently. Stir in half the sugar and stir until dissolved, pour into a large bowl. Beat in eggs, remaining sugar and vanilla extract.

◊ Into a small bowl, sift together flour, instant espresso powder, baking powder and salt. Stir into chocolate mixture until blended; then stir in pecans or walnuts and chocolate chips.

◊ Using an ice-cream scoop or ¼-cup measure, drop dough onto prepared baking sheets at least 3 inches apart. Flatten slightly with the back of a moistened spoon. Insert 5 pecans into edge of each cookie, to represent head and legs of a turtle. Bake, one sheet at a time, in center of oven until surface of cookies begins to split, about 10 minutes. (Do not overbake; the cookies should be soft in the center.) Remove baking sheets to wire rack to cool slightly. Then gently peel off foil or paper and remove cookies to wire racks to cool completely. Repeat with remaining dough and nuts. Store in airtight containers.

17

OATMEAL LACE

ABOVE & BELOW

ABOUT 2 DOZEN

These beautiful lacy cookies are so thin they are transparent, but simple to make.

INGREDIENTS

◊ 1½ cups quick-cooking rolled oats

◊ 1 cup packed light brown sugar

◊ ½ cup sugar

◊ 2 tbsp all-purpose flour

◊ ¼ tsp salt

◊ ⅔ cup (1 stick) plus 2⅔ tbsp unsalted butter, melted

◊ 1 egg, lightly beaten

◊ 1 tsp vanilla extract

◊ ½ cup mini chocolate chips

◊ Preheat oven to 350°F. In a large bowl, combine oats, sugars, flour and salt. Make a well in center and add the melted butter, egg and vanilla extract. Stir until well-blended and soft batter-like dough forms; stir in chocolate chips.

◊ Drop half-teaspoonfuls, 2½ inches apart, on ungreased baking sheets. Bake 3 to 5 minutes until edges are lightly browned and centers bubbling; cookies will spread to large disks. Remove baking sheets to wire racks to cool slightly.

◊ When edges are firm enough to lift, use a thin palette knife to remove cookies to wire racks to cool completely. Repeat with remaining batter. Cookies can be stored in airtight containers with waxed paper between the layers. They are crisp and fragile.

BROWNIE COOKIES

NOT ILLUSTRATED

ABOUT 3 DOZEN

This soft chewy chocolate cookie is like a brownie. Do not overbake or it will be dry.

INGREDIENTS

◊ ⅔ cup all-purpose flour

◊ ¼ tsp salt

◊ 2 oz (2 squares) unsweetened chocolate, chopped

◊ ½ cup (1 stick) unsalted butter, softened

◊ 1 cup sugar

◊ 2 eggs, lightly beaten

◊ 1 tsp vanilla extract

◊ ¾ cup chopped walnuts

◊ ¾ cup semisweet chocolate chips

◊ confectioners' sugar for dusting

◊ Preheat oven to 350°F. Grease 2 baking sheets. Into a small bowl, sift together flour and salt; set aside.

◊ In a heat-proof bowl placed over a saucepan of simmering water, melt chocolate, stirring frequently, until smooth. Remove from heat to cool slightly. In a large bowl with electric mixer, beat butter until creamy, about 30 seconds. Add sugar and beat until light and fluffy, 1 to 2 minutes. Beat in eggs and vanilla extract; then stir in walnuts and chocolate chips. Add flour mixture and stir until just blended.

◊ Drop tablespoonfuls, 2 inches apart, onto greased baking sheets, and bake until tops feel set but centers remain moist, about 10 to 12 minutes. Remove baking sheets to wire racks to cool until cookies have set and become firm enough to move, about 5 minutes. Then, using a metal pancake turner or palette knife, remove cookies to wire rack to cool completely. Repeat with remaining cookie mixture.

◊ Dust cooled cookies with a little confectioners' sugar. Store in airtight containers with waxed paper between the layers.

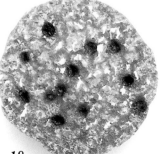

Muesli Cookies

LEFT & BELOW

ABOUT 3 DOZEN

These chewy cookies are sturdy enough to send in the mail or take on a picnic. They keep well, if they last that long.

INGREDIENTS

◊ 2¼ cups all-purpose flour

◊ 2½ tsp baking powder

◊ 2 tsp ground cinnamon

◊ ½ tsp ground nutmeg

◊ ½ tsp baking soda

◊ ½ tsp salt

◊ ½ cup (1 stick) unsalted butter, softened

◊ 1 cup sugar

◊ ¼ cup fresh orange juice

◊ 1 egg

◊ 1 cup natural unsweetened muesli cereal

◊ ½ cup raisins

◊ ½ cup chopped walnuts or almonds

◊ ½ cup quick-cooking oats

◊ Preheat oven to 250°F. Lightly grease 2 large baking sheets. Into a medium bowl, sift together flour, baking powder, cinnamon, nutmeg, baking soda and salt.

◊ In a large bowl with electric mixer, beat butter and sugar until light and fluffy, 1 to 2 minutes. Slowly beat in orange juice and egg. Stir in flour mixture until well-blended; then stir in muesli cereal, raisins, chopped nuts and oats.

◊ Drop rounded tablespoonfuls at least 2 inches apart onto prepared baking sheets. Smooth tops slightly with moistened fingertip. Bake until surface is set and lightly browned, 15 to 18 minutes, rotating baking sheets from top to bottom shelf and front to back halfway through cooking time. Remove baking sheets to wire racks to cool slightly. Then, using a metal pancake turner or palette knife, remove cookies to wire racks to cool completely. Repeat with remaining dough. Store in airtight containers.

CHOCOLATE-NUT CHEWIES

NOT ILLUSTRATED

ABOUT 3 DOZEN

This cookie is almost all nuts, fruit and chocolate.
They are soft and chewy and don't last long.

INGREDIENTS

◊ 1 cup unblanched whole almonds

◊ ¾ cup pecan or walnut halves

◊ ¾ cup blanched hazelnuts

◊ 1 cup all-purpose flour

◊ 1 tsp baking soda

◊ ¼ tsp salt

◊ ½ cup (1 stick) unsalted butter, softened

◊ ½ cup sugar

◊ ¼ cup packed light brown sugar

◊ 1 egg

◊ 1 tsp vanilla extract

◊ 1 cup semisweet chocolate chips

◊ 1 cup raisins

◊ ½ cup golden raisins

◊ Preheat oven to 375°F. Place nuts on a large baking sheet and toast until golden and fragrant, 5 to 7 minutes, stirring and shaking baking sheet occasionally. Pour onto a plate and cool completely, then chop coarsely.

◊ Into a small bowl, sift together flour, baking soda and salt. In a large mixing bowl with electric mixer, beat butter until creamy, about 30 seconds. Add sugars and beat until light and fluffy; 1 to 2 more minutes. Beat in egg and vanilla extract. Stir in flour mixture until blended; then stir in chocolate chips, raisins, golden raisins and nuts until evenly distributed.

◊ Drop heaped tablespoonfuls, at least 2 inches apart, onto 2 large ungreased baking sheets. Bake until set and golden, 12 to 15 minutes, rotating baking sheets from top to bottom shelf and front to back halfway through cooking time. Remove baking sheets to wire racks to cool slightly. Then, using a metal pancake turner or palette knife, remove cookies to wire racks to cool completely. Repeat with the remaining mixture. Store in airtight containers.

MAPLE-PECAN WAFERS

NOT ILLUSTRATED

ABOUT 2 DOZEN

These elegant cookies are ideal served with ice cream. Make an effort to find real natural maple syrup, not the artificial flavoring – it makes a big difference.

INGREDIENTS

◊ 2 cups pecan halves

◊ ¼ cup (½ stick) unsalted butter

◊ 1¼ cups packed light brown sugar

◊ ⅓ cup all-purpose flour

◊ 1 tsp natural maple flavor

◊ ¼ tsp salt

◊ 1 egg, lightly beaten

◊ Preheat oven to 350°F. Line a large baking sheet with foil. Set aside 24 perfect pecan halves, then chop remaining nuts.

◊ In a medium saucepan over low heat, melt butter. Remove from heat and stir in brown sugar, flour, maple flavor, salt and beaten egg until well-blended. Drop tablespoonfuls, at least 3 inches apart, onto foil-lined sheet. Place a reserved pecan half onto center of each.

◊ Bake cookies 12 minutes. Remove baking sheet to wire rack to cool slightly. Slide foil with cookies onto wire rack to cool completely. Cool baking sheet, and reline with foil to repeat with remaining cookie mixture and pecans. (You can use another baking sheet, which can be prepared in advance, but bake cookies one sheet at a time, not in layers.) When cookies are cold, peel off foil and store in airtight containers with waxed paper between layers.

SWEDISH ALMOND WAFERS

BELOW & RIGHT

ABOUT 2 DOZEN

Grinding your own almonds makes all the
difference to these rich, buttery, lacelike cookies.
Be sure to leave lots of space between the cookies
as they really spread. Having extra baking sheets is
helpful as it is necessary to bake them in small
batches.

INGREDIENTS

◊ ¾ cup unblanched almonds

◊ ½ cup superfine sugar

◊ ½ cup (1 stick) unsalted
butter, cut into pieces

◊ 2 tbsp all-purpose flour

◊ ¼ tsp salt

◊ 2 tbsp light cream

◊ Preheat oven to 350°F. Lightly grease 2 large baking
sheets. In a food processor fitted with metal blade,
process almonds until very finely ground. Do not
overgrind or they will form a paste. Add a little sugar,
and pulse again to be sure they are evenly ground.

◊ Combine almond mixture, remaining sugar, butter,
flour, salt and cream in a heavy-based saucepan, and
cook over medium heat until butter is melted and batter
is smooth. Remove from heat.

◊ Drop scant teaspoonfuls, 3 to 4 inches apart, onto
baking sheets (you may only get 5 to 6 on a sheet). Bake
3 to 5 minutes, until lightly brown at the edges, but
bubbling in the center. Remove baking sheet to wire
racks to cool slightly.

◊ When edges are firm enough to lift, use a thin palette
knife to remove cookies to wire racks to cool completely.
Repeat with remaining batter, cooling and
regreasing baking sheets between each batch.
Cookies can be stored in airtight containers
with waxed paper between layers. They
are very fragile.

ALMOND MACAROONS

NOT ILLUSTRATED

ABOUT 30

This is an authentic macaroon, made with almond paste, egg whites and sugar.

INGREDIENTS

◊ 8 oz (½ lb) almond paste, cut into pieces

◊ 1 cup superfine sugar

◊ 3 egg whites, at room temperature

◊ ⅓ cup confectioners' sugar

◊ 2 tbsp cake flour

◊ ⅛ tsp salt

◊ 2 tbsp chopped blanched almonds

◊ Preheat oven to 300°F. Line 2 baking sheets with rice paper or lightly oiled non-stick parchment paper.

◊ In a food processor fitted with metal blade, using pulse action, process almond paste. Gradually add sugar and egg whites, and process until smooth. Sprinkle over confectioners' sugar, flour and salt, and, using pulse action, process until well-blended. Scrape into a bowl and chill 15 minutes to firm slightly.

◊ Drop teaspoonfuls, 2 inches apart, onto prepared baking sheets, and sprinkle a few chopped almonds onto center of each mound. Cover with a clean dish cloth, and allow to sit 30 minutes. Bake until pale golden and set, about 20 to 25 minutes.

◊ Dampen 2 dish cloths, and spread over 2 wire racks. Remove baking sheets from oven, and slide paper linings onto the damp cloths. Allow to cool completely, then peel macaroons off paper.

TIPS

Almond paste is a commercially prepared paste of ground almonds and is available at most large supermarkets.

Rice paper is an edible paper available in cookware and specialty shops.

LUXURY MACAROONS

LEFT & ABOVE

2 DOZEN

The macadamias are a new addition and go very well with coconut.

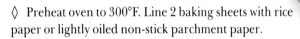

INGREDIENTS

◊ 3 cups sweetened, flaked coconut

◊ 1 cup unsalted macadamia nuts, chopped

◊ flavorless vegetable oil for greasing

◊ ⅔ cup sweetened condensed milk

◊ 1 tsp vanilla extract

◊ 2 egg whites

◊ pinch of salt

◊ 6 oz white or semisweet chocolate, melted (optional)

◊ Preheat oven to 350°F. Place flaked coconut on 1 large baking sheet and macadamia nuts on another. Toast until lightly golden, 7 to 10 minutes, stirring and shaking frequently. Pour coconut onto one plate and nuts onto another to cool completely.

◊ Line 2 large baking sheets with non-stick baking parchment. Brush very lightly with oil. Into a large bowl, combine condensed milk, vanilla extract, flaked coconut and macadamia nuts until well-blended.

◊ In a medium bowl with electric mixer on medium speed, beat egg whites until foamy. Add salt and increase mixer speed to high. Continue beating until whites are stiff but not dry. Fold whites into coconut mixture. Drop rounded tablespoonfuls onto prepared baking sheets. Bake until golden around edges, 12 to 14 minutes. Remove baking sheets to wire racks to cool completely, then gently peel off paper.

◊ Line a large baking sheet with waxed paper. Dip macaroon bottoms into melted white or semisweet chocolate. Place on lined cookie sheet until chocolate sets, 15 to 20 minutes. Peel off paper and refrigerate in airtight containers with waxed paper between layers.

SPICY APPLESAUCE COOKIES

ABOVE & BELOW

ABOUT 3 DOZEN

These soft spicy cookies are delicious. If you don't like nuts, substitute some chopped dates.

INGREDIENTS

◊ ½ cup (1 stick) unsalted butter, softened

◊ ½ cup packed light brown sugar

◊ ⅓ cup sugar

◊ 1 egg

◊ 1 cup applesauce

◊ 2 cups all-purpose flour

◊ 1 tsp baking soda

◊ ½ tsp salt

◊ 1 tsp ground cinnamon

◊ 1 tsp ground ginger

◊ ½ tsp ground cloves

◊ 1 cup golden raisins

◊ ¾ cup chopped walnuts or pecans

◊ ¾ cup semisweet chocolate chips

◊ Preheat the oven to 350°F. Lightly grease 2 large baking sheets. In a large bowl with electric mixer, beat butter until creamy, about 30 seconds. Add sugars, and beat until light and fluffy, 1 to 2 minutes. Beat in egg, and stir in applesauce.

◊ Into a medium bowl, sift together flour, baking soda, salt, cinnamon, ginger and cloves. Stir into butter-sugar mixture until well-blended; then stir in raisins, walnuts or pecans and chocolate chips.

◊ Drop tablespoonfuls, about 1½ inches apart, onto baking sheets. Bake until golden, 5 to 7 minutes. Remove baking sheets to wire racks to cool slightly. Using a metal pancake turner or palette knife, remove cookies to wire rack to cool completely. Repeat with remaining mixture. Store in airtight containers.

> **TIP**
> *I*f you like, press a walnut on top of each cookie before baking.

24

SPICY MOLASSES DROPS

NOT ILLUSTRATED

ABOUT 40

These cookies are small but packed with a rich, spicy flavor.

INGREDIENTS

◊ 1 cup all-purpose flour

◊ 1 tsp ground cinnamon

◊ ½ tsp ground ginger

◊ ½ tsp ground nutmeg

◊ ¼ tsp ground cloves

◊ ½ tsp baking soda

◊ ½ tsp salt

◊ ¼ cup butter or margarine, softened

◊ ¼ cup white vegetable shortening

◊ ¼ cup molasses

◊ ¾ cup packed dark brown sugar

◊ 1 egg

GLAZE

◊ 1 cup confectioners' sugar, sifted

◊ 3 tsp water

◊ ½ tsp vanilla extract

◊ Preheat oven to 375°F. Into a medium bowl, sift together flour, cinnamon, ginger, nutmeg, cloves, baking soda and salt. In a large bowl with electric mixer, beat butter or margarine, shortening, molasses, brown sugar and egg until well-blended, 2 to 3 minutes. Stir in flour-spice mixture until well-blended.

◊ Drop teaspoonfuls, 1 inch apart, onto 2 large ungreased baking sheets. Bake until crisp and golden, 7 to 10 minutes. Remove baking sheets to wire racks to cool slightly. Then, using a metal pancake turner, remove cookies to wire rack to cool completely. Repeat with remaining cookie mixture.

◊ In a small bowl, mix confectioners' sugar, water and vanilla extract to form a glaze. Arrange cookies on a rack over a baking sheet (to catch drips), and drizzle with glaze. Allow glaze to dry completely. Store in airtight containers.

MAPLE WALNUT DROPS

NOT ILLUSTRATED

ABOUT 4 DOZEN

INGREDIENTS

◊ 1 cup raisins

◊ 2½ cups all-purpose flour

◊ 1 tsp salt

◊ ¾ tsp baking powder

◊ ¼ tsp baking soda

◊ 1 tsp ground cinnamon

◊ ½ tsp ground nutmeg

◊ ¾ cup (1½ sticks) unsalted butter, softened

◊ 1 cup packed light brown sugar

◊ 2 eggs

◊ ¾ tsp natural maple flavor

◊ ⅓ cup cold, strong black coffee

◊ 1½ cups coarsely chopped walnuts

◊ In a small bowl, cover raisins with hot water, stand 15 minutes to plump. Drain and pat dry; set aside. Into a medium bowl, sift together flour, salt, baking powder, baking soda, cinnamon and nutmeg; set aside.

◊ In a large bowl with electric mixer, beat butter until creamy, about 30 seconds. Add brown sugar and continue beating until light and fluffy, 1 to 2 minutes. Beat in eggs, one at a time, beating well after each addition. Beat in maple flavor.

◊ In 3 batches, add flour mixture and black coffee beginning and ending with flour mixture. If mixture seems too stiff, add a little more coffee or water, but mixture should be stiff enough to drop. Stir in walnuts and raisins. Refrigerate dough until chilled, 30 minutes.

◊ Preheat oven to 350°F. Lightly grease 2 large baking sheets. Drop dough by heaping teaspoonfuls, 2 inches apart, onto prepared baking sheets. (Keep remaining cookie dough refrigerated.) Bake until golden and firm to the touch, 13 to 15 minutes, rotating baking sheets from top to bottom shelf and front to back halfway through cooking time. Remove baking sheets to wire racks to cool slightly; then, using a metal pancake turner or palette knife, remove cookies to wire racks to cool completely. Repeat with remaining dough. Store in airtight containers.

SESAME WAFERS

LEFT & BELOW

ABOUT 3 DOZEN

These are sweet crisp wafers, rich with the flavor of sesame and very easy to make in a skillet.

INGREDIENTS

◊ ½ cup sesame seeds
◊ 1 tbsp butter
◊ 1 cup packed light brown sugar
◊ 3 tbsp all-purpose flour
◊ 1 egg, lightly beaten
◊ 1 tsp vanilla extract
◊ pinch of salt

◊ Preheat oven to 350°F. Grease well 2 large baking sheets. In a medium skillet, over medium heat, toast sesame seeds, stirring and shaking skillet until they are golden brown. Remove skillet from the heat, cool slightly, then stir in remaining ingredients until well-blended.

◊ Drop teaspoonfuls, 2½ inches apart, onto the greased baking sheets (the wafers will spread). Bake 3 to 5 minutes until just golden-brown. Remove baking sheets to wire racks to cool slightly.

◊ When edges are firm enough to lift, use a thin palette knife to remove cookies to wire racks to cool completely. Repeat with remaining mixture, cooling and regreasing baking sheets between each batch. Cookies can be stored in airtight containers with waxed paper between each layer. They are crisp and fragile.

DOUBLE CHOCOLATE CHIP COOKIES

NOT ILLUSTRATED

ABOUT 4 DOZEN

This is a slightly updated version of the classic chocolate chip cookie – more chunky than ever.

INGREDIENTS

◊ 2¼ cups all-purpose flour
◊ 1 tsp baking soda
◊ ¾ tsp salt
◊ 1 cup unsalted butter or margarine, softened
◊ 1 cup packed light brown sugar
◊ ½ cup sugar
◊ 2 eggs
◊ 1 tsp vanilla extract
◊ 12 oz semisweet chocolate chips or semisweet chocolate chopped into small pieces
◊ 6 oz fine-quality white chocolate chopped into small pieces
◊ 1 cup chopped pecans or walnuts

◊ Preheat oven to 375°F. Into a large bowl, sift together flour, baking soda and salt. In a large bowl with electric mixer, beat butter and sugars until light and fluffy. With mixer on low speed, beat in eggs, beating well after each addition, and scraping down sides of bowl occasionally. Beat in vanilla extract; then stir in flour mixture until well-mixed. Stir in chocolate chips and nuts.

◊ Drop rounded tablespoonfuls, at least 2 inches apart, onto 2 large ungreased baking sheets. Bake until set and golden-brown, 10 to 13 minutes, rotating baking sheets from top to bottom shelf and front to back halfway through cooking time. Remove baking sheets to wire racks to cool slightly; then using a metal pancake turner or palette knife, remove cookies to wire racks to cool completely. Repeat with remaining cookie dough. Store in airtight containers.

TRIPLE CHOCOLATE CHUNK COOKIES

ABOVE & RIGHT

ABOUT 18

These cookies are large and flat, crisp on the edge and soft in the center and filled with chocolate – a chocolate lover's dream. For best results, do not overbake.

INGREDIENTS

◊ 9 oz bittersweet or semisweet chocolate, chopped

◊ ¾ cup (1½ sticks) unsalted butter, cut into pieces

◊ 3 eggs

◊ ¾ cup sugar

◊ ⅓ cup packed light brown sugar

◊ 2 tsp vanilla extract

◊ ½ cup all-purpose flour

◊ 6 tbsp cocoa powder, sifted

◊ 1½ tsp baking powder

◊ ¼ tsp salt

◊ 9 oz semisweet chocolate, chopped into ¼-in. pieces or 1½ cups semisweet chocolate chips

◊ 6 oz fine-quality milk chocolate, chopped into ¼-in. pieces

◊ 6 oz fine-quality white chocolate, chopped into ¼-in. pieces

◊ 1½ cups pecans or walnuts, toasted and chopped

◊ Preheat oven to 325°F. Lightly grease 2 large baking sheets. In a medium saucepan over low heat, melt bittersweet or semisweet chocolate and butter, stirring frequently until smooth. Remove from heat to cool slightly.

◊ In a large bowl with electric mixer, beat eggs and sugars until light and fluffy, about 2 to 3 minutes. On low speed, gradually beat in melted chocolate and vanilla extract until well-blended. Into a small bowl, sift together flour, cocoa powder, baking powder and salt; then gently stir into chocolate mixture. Stir in unmelted chocolate pieces and nuts.

◊ Drop heaped tablespoonfuls, at least 4 inches apart, onto baking sheets. Moisten the bottom of a drinking glass, and flatten each dough round slightly, trying to make each cookie about 3 inches round; you will only fit 4 to 6 cookies on each baking sheet. Bake 10 minutes until tops are cracked and shiny; do not overbake or cookies will break when removed from baking sheet.

◊ Remove baking sheets to wire racks to cool slightly. Then, using a metal pancake turner or palette knife, carefully remove cookies to wire rack to cool completely. Repeat with remaining cookie dough. Store in airtight containers.

27

TRIPLE CHOCOLATE PEANUT BUTTER COOKIES

NOT ILLUSTRATED

ABOUT 18

There is hardly any cookie to hold together the chunks of chocolate and nuts – handle them with care.

INGREDIENTS

◊ 1 cup all-purpose flour

◊ ¾ tsp baking soda

◊ ½ cup (1 stick) unsalted butter, softened

◊ ½ cup smooth peanut butter

◊ 1 tsp vanilla extract

◊ ½ cup firmly packed light brown sugar

◊ ½ cup sugar

◊ 1 egg, lightly beaten

◊ 4 oz semisweet chocolate, chopped into ¼-in pieces

◊ 4 oz milk chocolate, chopped into ¼-in pieces

◊ 4 oz fine-quality white chocolate, chopped into ¼-in pieces

◊ 1 cup salted peanuts

◊ Preheat oven to 350°F. Line 2 large baking sheets with foil, shiny side up. Into a small bowl, sift together the flour and baking soda.

◊ In a large bowl with electric mixer, beat butter, peanut butter and vanilla extract until smooth and creamy, 1 to 2 minutes, scraping bowl occasionally. Add sugars and beat 1 minute more; then beat in egg until well-blended. Reduce mixer speed to low, and beat in flour mixture until just blended. Stir in chopped chocolates and peanuts; dough will be very stiff.

◊ Using an ice-cream scoop or ¼-cup measure, scoop up cookie dough, flatten bottom against side of bowl and drop, 3 inches apart, onto foil-lined baking sheets. Moisten bottom of a drinking glass, and flatten each mound to about ¾-inch thickness.

◊ Bake until slightly puffed but barely colored, 17 to 20 minutes, rotating baking sheets from top to bottom shelf and front to back halfway through cooking time. The cookies will feel very soft to the touch and flatten as they cool. Remove baking sheets to wire racks and cool until cookies are firm enough to move, 7 to 10 minutes. Then, using a wide metal pancake turner, remove cookies to wire racks to cool completely. Repeat with remaining cookie dough. Cookies are very fragile; they can be stored in large airtight containers with waxed paper between layers.

TIP

Cookie dough can be scooped onto sheets of foil all at once, and set aside; then slid onto cooled baking sheets as they are cooled.

NEW ENGLAND-STYLE JUMBLES

LEFT, RIGHT & BELOW

ABOUT 3 DOZEN

This is a new version of an old-fashioned
American cookie which was so called because of
the nuts "jumbled" into the dough.

INGREDIENTS

◊ 1¼ cups all-purpose flour

◊ ¾ tsp baking soda

◊ ½ tsp ground cinnamon

◊ ⅛ tsp salt

◊ 1 cup semisweet chocolate
chips

◊ ¾ cup walnuts, coarsely
chopped

◊ ¾ cup hazelnuts, chopped

◊ ¾ cup unblanched whole
almonds, chopped

◊ 1 cup dried cranberries

◊ ½ cup dried cherries

◊ ½ cup unsalted butter,
softened

◊ ¾ cup sugar

◊ ¼ cup packed light brown
sugar

◊ 1 egg

◊ 1 tsp vanilla extract

◊ Preheat oven to 375°F. Into a medium bowl, sift
together flour, baking soda, cinnamon and salt. In a
large bowl, stir chocolate chips, walnuts, hazelnuts,
almonds, cranberries and cherries.

◊ In a large bowl with electric mixer, beat butter until
creamy, 30 seconds. Add sugars and beat until light and
fluffy, 1 to 2 minutes. Beat in egg and vanilla extract. On
low speed, beat in flour mixture until blended. Pour into
bowl of nuts and dried fruits, and stir until combined.

◊ Drop rounded tablespoonfuls, 2 inches
apart, on 2 large ungreased baking sheets.
Bake until golden, 12 to 15 minutes,
rotating baking sheets from top to
bottom shelf and from front to
back halfway through cooking
time. Remove baking sheets to
wire racks to cool slightly. Then
remove cookies to wire racks to
cool completely. Repeat with
remaining cookie dough.

> **TIP**
> *I*f dough seems
> soft, refrigerate
> 15 minutes before
> dropping onto
> baking sheets. This
> will keep batter
> from spreading
> too much.

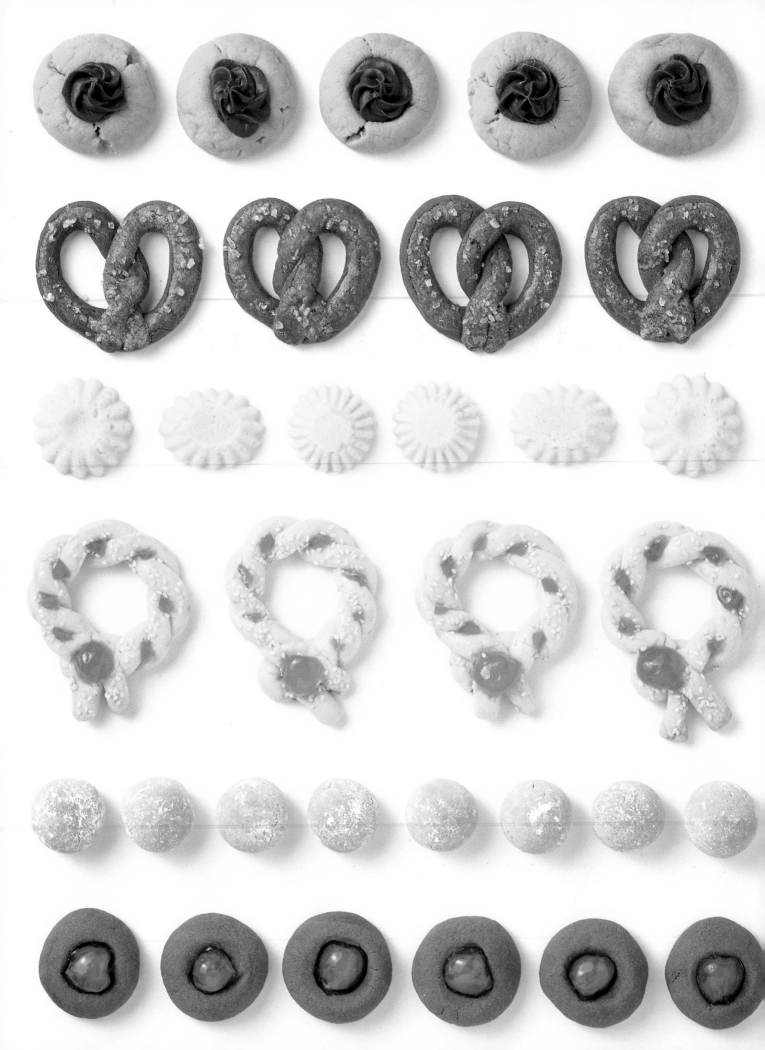

2

MOLDED
Cookies

These cookies can be shaped

into balls, logs, or cylinders with the hands,

or formed using special molds.

Pine Nut Macaroons

Mocha Nut Cookies

Chocolate Pretzel Cookies

Italian Almond Cookies

Kourambiedes

Austrian Crescents

Light and Lemony
Madeleines

Chocolate Madeleines

Cookie Jar Gingersnaps

Triple Nut Logs

Chocolate Butter Cookies

Chocolate Peanut Butter
Cookie-Cups

Peanut Butter Cookies

Mexican Wedding Cakes

Chinese Almond Cookies

Poppy Seed Pistachio Puffs

Triple Ginger Cookies

German Pepper Nuts

Cinnamon Balls

Chocolate-Dipped Hazelnut
Crescents

Almond and Pine Nut Biscotti

Greek Christmas Wreaths

Chocolate-Nut Biscotti

Sandkakers

Snickerdoodles

Cookie Candy Canes

Rich Cardamom Cookies

PINE NUT MACAROONS

RIGHT & BELOW

ABOUT 2 DOZEN

In Italy, pine nut macaroons are often sandwiched together with a little apricot preserve – delicious.

INGREDIENTS

◊ 3 tbsp dried currants

◊ 3 tbsp Marsala wine

◊ ¾ cup slivered blanched almonds, lightly toasted

◊ ½ cup pine nuts, lightly toasted

◊ ½ cup superfine sugar

◊ 1 tbsp all-purpose flour

◊ 1 egg white

◊ ¼ tsp almond extract

◊ 1 cup pine nuts

◊ Preheat oven to 350°F. Line a large baking sheet with foil (shiny side up) or non-stick baking parchment. In a small bowl, combine dried currants and Marsala, and microwave on high (100% power), 30 to 60 seconds. Allow to sit until moisture is evaporated, 3 to 5 minutes. Cool completely.

◊ In a food processor fitted with metal blade, process the toasted almonds, pine nuts, sugar and flour until finely ground. Add egg white and almond extract, and process until mixture forms a dough. Turn into a bowl, and stir in the plumped currants.

◊ Into a pie plate, place untoasted pine nuts. Wet your hands, and, using a teaspoon to scoop out dough, shape dough into ¾-inch balls. Roll balls in pine nuts, pressing lightly to cover completely. Place balls 1½ inches apart on lined baking sheet; flatten slightly to a disc shape.

◊ Bake cookies until pine nuts are golden, 12 to 15 minutes, rotating baking sheet front to back halfway through cooking time. Remove baking sheet to wire rack to cool, 2 to 3 minutes. Then, using a metal pancake turner or palette knife, remove cookies to wire rack to cool; completely. Store in airtight containers.

MOCHA NUT COOKIES

NOT ILLUSTRATED

ABOUT 3 DOZEN

These cookies combine hazelnuts, chocolate and coffee to make a delicious cookie especially with a cup of coffee.

INGREDIENTS

◊ 1 cup all-purpose flour

◊ 1¼ cups hazelnuts, toasted, husked and finely ground

◊ 1 oz bittersweet or semisweet chocolate, grated

◊ ¼ tsp salt

◊ ½ tsp ground cinnamon

◊ ½ cup (1 stick) unsalted butter, softened

◊ ¼ cup superfine sugar

◊ 1 tbsp instant espresso or coffee powder, dissolved in 2 tsp hot water

◊ whole blanched hazelnuts, toasted (about 3 dozen) for decoration

◊ ½ cup confectioners' sugar

◊ 1 tbsp cocoa powder

◊ ½ tsp ground cinnamon

◊ Preheat oven to 325°F. In a medium bowl, combine flour, hazelnuts, chocolate, salt and cinnamon. Set aside.

◊ In a large bowl with electric mixer, beat butter until creamy, 30 seconds. Add sugar and continue beating until light and fluffy. Beat in dissolved espresso or coffee powder. On low speed, gradually add flour-nut mixture until well-blended.

◊ Using 2 teaspoonfuls of dough for each cookie, shape dough into balls and place, 2 inches apart, on 2 large ungreased baking sheets. Press a whole hazelnut into center of each ball. Bake cookies until just golden, 12 to 15 minutes. Remove baking sheets to wire racks to cool slightly. Then, using a metal pancake turner, remove cookies to wire racks to cool completely.

◊ Arrange cookies on a wire rack over a sheet of waxed paper. Into a small bowl, sift confectioners' sugar, cocoa powder and cinnamon. Dust cookies with sugar mixture. Store in airtight containers.

CHOCOLATE PRETZEL COOKIES

ABOVE & BELOW

ABOUT 30

These chocolate cookies are surprisingly easy to form; just be sure to chill the dough long enough.

INGREDIENTS

◊ 1¼ cup all-purpose flour

◊ ¼ tsp salt

◊ 3 tbsp unsweetened cocoa powder

◊ ½ cup (1 stick) unsalted butter, softened

◊ ⅔ cup superfine sugar

◊ 1 egg, lightly beaten

◊ 1 tsp vanilla extract

GLAZE

◊ 1 egg white, lightly beaten

◊ sugar crystals, for sprinkling

◊ Lightly grease 2 large baking sheets. Into a medium bowl, sift together flour, salt, and cocoa powder. In a large bowl, beat butter until creamy, 30 seconds. Add sugar and continue beating until light and fluffy, 1 to 2 minutes. Beat in egg and vanilla extract until well-blended. On low speed, gradually add flour until blended. Turn dough onto a piece of plastic wrap and shape into a ball; flatten to a disk shape and wrap tightly. Refrigerate until firm, about 1 hour.

◊ Preheat oven to 375°F. With lightly floured hands, roll dough into about 30 1½-inch balls. On a lightly floured surface, roll each dough ball into a "rope" about 9 inches long. Bring each end of "rope" to meet in center. Twist the ends together, and press to middle of rope to form pretzel shape. Transfer to greased baking sheets.

◊ Brush each cookie with egg white to glaze; then sprinkle with sugar crystals. Bake until pretzels feel firm, 10 to 12 minutes. Remove baking sheets to wire racks; cool slightly until firm enough to move. Then remove cookies to wire racks to cool. Store in airtight containers.

> **TIP**
> If dough becomes too soft to handle, return to the refrigerator for a few minutes to firm then continue shaping dough.

ITALIAN ALMOND COOKIES

ABOUT 3 ½ DOZEN

These cookies are adapted from the *ricciarelli di Siena* – a rich, soft, chewy macaroon. They use almond flour, available at specialty food shops.

INGREDIENTS

◊ 2 egg whites

◊ ⅛ tsp cream of tartar

◊ 1¼ cups superfine sugar

◊ grated zest of 1 lemon or orange

◊ 1 tsp vanilla extract

◊ ½ tsp almond extract

◊ 3 cups almond flour

◊ ¼ cup all-purpose flour

◊ blanched almonds to decorate

◊ confectioners' sugar

◊ Preheat oven to 250°F. Lightly grease 2 large non-stick baking sheets.

◊ In a large bowl with electric mixer, beat whites until foamy. Add cream of tartar and continue beating until soft peaks form. Gradually beat in 1 cup of the sugar, 1 tablespoon at a time, beating well after each addition. Continue beating until whites are stiff and glossy. (This will take at least 10 minutes.) Fold in lemon or orange zest, vanilla and almond extracts, and almond flour until stiff dough forms.

◊ In a small bowl, combine remaining sugar and the all-purpose flour. Lightly dust the greased baking sheets and your work surface with remaining mixture.

◊ Using lightly oiled hands, divide dough into quarters. Roll each quarter into a long log about 1 inch in diameter; using fingertips, flatten slightly. Using an oiled knife, cut logs into 1-inch pieces, and arrange on baking sheets 1 inch apart. Press an almond in the center of each cookie. (You may need to bake in batches.)

◊ Bake until cookies are set and lightly puffed, about 15 to 17 minutes (cookies should be very pale), rotating baking sheets from top to bottom shelf and from front to back, halfway through cooking time. Remove baking sheets to wire racks, dust with confectioners' sugar then cool completely. Store in airtight containers.

KOURAMBIEDES

ABOUT 3 DOZEN

These rich, tender almond cookies are served at all festive occasions in Greece. At Christmas, they often bury a whole clove in the cookie to symbolize the gifts the three wise men brought to the Christ-child.

INGREDIENTS

◊ ½ cup blanched almonds, lightly toasted and cooled

◊ 1 cup (2 sticks) unsalted butter, softened

◊ 2 tbsp confectioners' sugar

◊ ¼ tsp salt

◊ 1 small egg yolk

◊ 1 tbsp brandy or orange-flavor liqueur

◊ 2 cups cake flour, sifted

◊ confectioners' sugar for dusting

◊ Preheat oven to 450°F. In a food processor fitted with metal blade, process cooled, toasted almonds until very fine crumbs form.

◊ In a medium bowl with electric mixer, beat butter until creamy, 30 seconds. Gradually add sugar and continue beating until light and fluffy, 1 to 2 minutes. Beat in salt, egg yolk and brandy. On low speed, gradually beat in cake flour and ground almonds until a soft dough forms. Scrape bowl and refrigerate until firm, about 1 hour.

◊ Use a tablespoon to scoop out dough, and form into 1-inch balls. Place on ungreased baking sheets, and bake until set and just golden, 15 to 20 minutes. Remove baking sheets to racks to cool slightly. Then, using a metal pancake turner or palette knife, remove cookies to wire racks to cool completely. Dust with confectioners' sugar. Store in airtight containers.

AUSTRIAN CRESCENTS

ABOVE & BELOW

ABOUT 3 DOZEN

This is a typical Viennese cookie. The addition of ground almonds makes the dough very short and they melt in your mouth.

INGREDIENTS

◊ ½ cup (1 stick) unsalted butter, softened

◊ 1 cup all-purpose flour

◊ ½ cup slivered blanched almonds, finely ground

◊ ¼ tsp salt

◊ ¾ tsp almond extract

◊ confectioners' sugar for dusting

◊ Preheat oven to 325°F. Grease 2 large baking sheets.

◊ In a large bowl, with electric mixer, beat butter until creamy, 30 seconds. On low speed, gradually beat in flour, ground almonds, salt and almond extract, until a soft dough forms.

◊ Using a teaspoon, scoop out dough and, using your lightly floured fingers, shape into 1½-inch crescents. Place crescents 1 inch apart on baking sheets. Bake until crescents are firm and just lightly golden (cookies should be pale), about 18 to 20 minutes, rotating from top to bottom shelf and from front to back halfway through cooking time.

◊ Remove baking sheets to wire racks to cool slightly. Then, using a metal pancake turner or palette knife, remove cookies to wire racks to cool completely. Arrange crescents on wire rack, and dust lightly with confectioners' sugar. Store in airtight containers. If you like, redust with confectioners' sugar before serving.

35

LIGHT AND LEMONY MADELEINES

ABOVE & BELOW

ABOUT 1 DOZEN

Madeleines are a French cookie-cake baked in pretty shell-shaped molds. They are delicious with tea or anytime.

INGREDIENTS

◊ 2 eggs

◊ ¾ cup confectioners' sugar

◊ grated zest of 1 large lemon

◊ 1 tbsp lemon juice

◊ 1 cup plus 1 tbsp all-purpose flour, sifted

◊ 1 tsp baking powder

◊ 6 tbsp (¾ stick) unsalted butter, melted and cooled

◊ confectioners' sugar for dusting

◊ Preheat oven to 375°F. Butter a 12-cup madeleine mold. In a large bowl with electric mixer, beat eggs and sugar until light and pale and a slowly falling ribbon forms when beaters are lifted from the bowl, 5 to 7 minutes. Gently fold in lemon zest and juice.

◊ Add baking powder to flour and beginning and ending with flour, alternately gently fold in flour and butter in 4 or 5 batches. Allow batter to rest for 10 minutes. Spoon batter into prepared molds.

◊ Bake until a toothpick inserted into center of a madeleine comes out clean, 12 to 15 minutes rotating mold from front to back, three-quarters through cooking time. Remove from oven, and turn madeleines out onto wire rack immediately. Allow to cool completely. Dust with confectioners' sugar. Store in airtight containers.

CHOCOLATE MADELEINES

NOT ILLUSTRATED

3 DOZEN

This version of the classic madeleine is made with cocoa powder for a rich chocolate flavor.

INGREDIENTS

◊ 4 tbsp unsweetened cocoa powder (preferably Dutch-processed)

◊ 3 tbsp hot water

◊ 3 eggs

◊ 1 cup superfine sugar

◊ 2 tsp vanilla extract

◊ 1¼ cups cake flour

◊ ¾ tsp baking powder

◊ ¼ tsp salt

◊ ¾ cup (1½ sticks) unsalted butter, softened

◊ confectioners' sugar for dusting

◊ Preheat oven to 350°F. Butter a 12-cup madeleine mold. In a small bowl, dissolve cocoa powder in hot water, until completely smooth. Set aside to cool; then beat in eggs, sugar, and vanilla extract. Continue beating until mixture is light and creamy, 2 to 3 minutes.

◊ Into a bowl, sift together flour, baking powder and salt. Add half chocolate-egg mixture and butter, and, on low speed, beat until well blended. Increase speed to medium, and beat 1 minute more until light. Fold in remaining chocolate-egg mixture in 2 batches.

◊ Using a small ladle or large spoon, fill madeleine cup molds almost full. Bake until a toothpick inserted in center of madeleine comes out clean, 10 to 12 minutes. Rotate molds from front to back halfway through.

◊ Remove molds to wire rack and unmold madeleines onto rack immediately. Cool molds, and repeat with remaining batter. Madeleines are best eaten within a day or two of baking, as they tend to dry out on storage. Store in airtight containers. Dust with confectioners' sugar before serving.

> **TIP**
>
> *T*o cool molds quickly, run back of molds under cold running water to chill. Wipe out and rebutter molds to continue baking.

COOKIE JAR GINGERSNAPS

LEFT & RIGHT

ABOUT 4 DOZEN

This was my favorite in the huge boxes of Christmas cookies my mother baked with her friend Charlotte – they are soft and very gingery.

INGREDIENTS

◊ 2 cups all-purpose flour

◊ 1 tbsp ground ginger

◊ 2 tsp baking soda

◊ 1½ tsp ground cinnamon

◊ ½ tsp ground cloves

◊ ½ tsp salt

◊ ¾ cup white vegetable shortening

◊ 1 cup sugar

◊ 1 egg

◊ ¼ cup molasses

◊ sugar for rolling

◊ Preheat oven to 350°F. Into a medium bowl, sift together flour, ginger, baking soda, cinnamon, cloves and salt.

◊ In a large bowl with electric mixer, beat shortening until soft, 1 minute. Gradually add sugar and continue beating until mixture is light and fluffy. Beat in egg and molasses until well-blended. Stir in flour mixture until completely mixed.

◊ Place a little sugar in a medium bowl. Scoop out heaping teaspoonfuls of mixture. Using your palms, roll into ¾-inch balls and drop into the sugar. Roll to cover the surface completely; then place balls 2 inches apart on ungreased baking sheets.

◊ Bake until cookies are slightly rounded and tops appear lightly browned and crackled. Remove baking sheets to wire racks to cool slightly. Then, using a metal pancake turner or palette knife, remove cookies to wire racks to cool completely. Repeat with remaining cookie dough and sugar. Store in airtight containers.

TRIPLE NUT LOGS

NOT ILLUSTRATED

ABOUT 4 DOZEN

These tender, sweet cookies contain 3 different kinds of nuts. Drizzled with chocolate, they are an excellent accompaniment to coffee.

INGREDIENTS

◊ ⅓ cup blanched almonds
◊ ⅓ cup pecan halves
◊ ⅓ cup hazelnuts, toasted and husked
◊ 2 cups all-purpose flour
◊ ½ tsp salt
◊ 1 cup (2 sticks) unsalted butter, softened
◊ 1 cup confectioners' sugar
◊ 2 tsp vanilla extract
◊ 1 tsp almond extract
◊ confectioners' sugar for coating
◊ 4 oz milk or semisweet chocolate, melted

◊ In a food processor fitted with metal blade, process nuts, flour, and salt until fine crumbs form; set aside.

◊ In a large bowl with electric beater, beat butter and confectioners' sugar until soft and creamy; beat in vanilla and almond extracts. On low speed, beat in flour-nut mixture until dough is soft and well-blended. Turn dough onto a piece of plastic wrap, and shape into a ball; flatten to a disc shape and wrap tightly. Refrigerate until firm, about 1 hour.

◊ Preheat oven to 350°F. Line 2 large baking sheets with non-stick parchment paper. Form 1-inch pieces of dough, and roll into 1½-inch log shapes. Place 1½ inches apart on lined baking sheets. Bake until just golden, about 15 minutes. Remove baking sheets to wire racks to cool, 1 to 2 minutes. Then, using a metal pancake turner or palette knife, remove cookies to wire racks.

◊ While cookies are still warm, place about 1 cup confectioners' sugar in a bowl and roll logs to coat completely; shake off excess. Arrange cookies on wire racks. Using a teaspoon or paper cone (page 14), drizzle logs with the melted chocolate in a decorative pattern. Allow to set 20 minutes. Store in airtight containers.

CHOCOLATE BUTTER COOKIES

ABOVE & BELOW

ABOUT 3 DOZEN

These rich chocolatey butter cookies can also be formed in a cookie press for specific shapes for special occasions.

INGREDIENTS

◊ 1½ cups all-purpose flour
◊ ¼ cup unsweetened cocoa powder (preferably Dutch-processed)
◊ ¼ cup salt
◊ ¾ cup (1½ sticks) unsalted butter, softened
◊ ½ cup superfine sugar
◊ 1 egg yolk
◊ 1 tsp almond or vanilla extract
◊ 2 oz semisweet chocolate
◊ ⅓ cup unblanched chopped almonds, toasted

◊ Preheat oven to 375°F. In a medium bowl, sift together flour, cocoa powder, and salt.

◊ In a large bowl, with electric mixture, beat butter until creamy, 30 seconds. Gradually add sugar and beat until light and fluffy, 1 to 2 minutes. Add egg yolk and almond or vanilla extract, and beat 1 minute more. Gradually stir in flour mixture until well-blended.

◊ Using a teaspoon to scoop dough and also using your palms, form dough into 2-inch logs. Place logs 1 inch apart on greased baking sheets. Bake cookies until just set, 7 to 9 minutes. Remove baking sheets to wire racks to cool slightly. Place cookies on wire rack to cool completely.

◊ Arrange cookie logs on a wire rack placed over a baking sheet to catch any drips. Using a teaspoon or paper cone (page 14), drizzle cookies with chocolate in a zigzag pattern; then sprinkle with a few chopped almonds. Allow to set. Store in airtight containers.

> **TIP**
> Cookies can be shaped into 1½-inch balls and decorated with half a candied cherry, or dusted with confectioners' sugar.

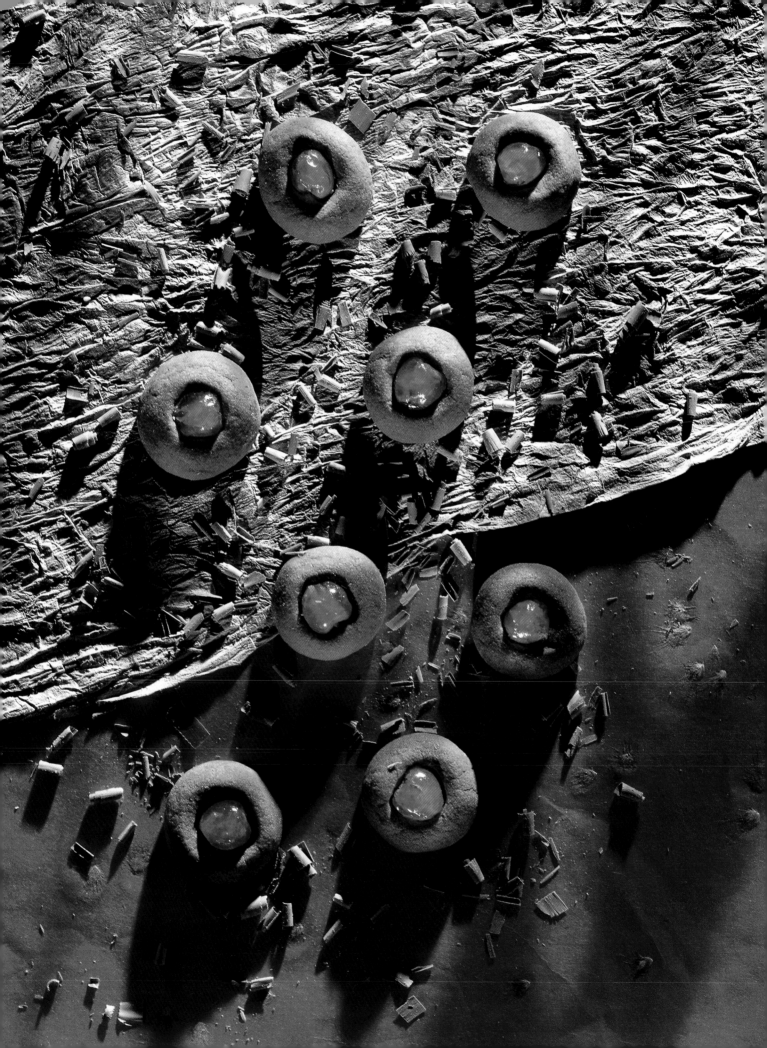

CHOCOLATE PEANUT-BUTTER COOKIE-CUPS

LEFT & BELOW

ABOUT 3 DOZEN

The combination of chocolate and peanut butter is a classic one.

INGREDIENTS

◊ 1 cup all-purpose flour

◊ 1 tsp baking powder

◊ ¼ tsp salt

◊ ½ cup (1 stick) unsalted butter, softened

◊ ½ cup packed light brown sugar

◊ ¼ cup sugar

◊ 1 cup smooth peanut butter

◊ 1 egg

◊ 1 tsp vanilla extract

CHOCOLATE FILLING

◊ 12 oz semisweet or bittersweet chocolate, chopped

◊ 6 tbsp (¾ stick) unsalted butter, softened

◊ Into a small bowl, sift together flour, baking powder and salt. In a large mixing bowl with electric mixer, beat butter until creamy, 30 seconds. Add sugars and continue beating until mixture is light and fluffy. Add peanut butter in 3 batches, beating well after each addition until mixture is well-blended. Beat in egg and vanilla extract. Stir in flour mixture until just mixed. Refrigerate the dough until chilled, 1 hour.

◊ Preheat oven to 375°F. Using a tablespoon, scoop out mixture and, using slightly moistened hands, roll between your palms to form 1-inch balls. Place balls 1½ inches apart on 2 ungreased baking sheets. Using a finger, press down into center to make a hole. Bake until just set and golden, 10 to 12 minutes. Rotate baking sheets halfway through cooking time. Remove baking sheets to wire racks to cool for about 2 to 3 minutes. Then remove cookies to wire rack to cool completely.

◊ In a medium bowl over a saucepan of simmering water, melt the chocolate until smooth, stirring frequently. Remove from heat, and cool slightly. Gently beat in butter until mixture just thickens. Spoon into a pastry bag fitted with a medium star tip. When cookies are completely cold, pipe a small amount of chocolate ganache into center of each cookie. Allow to set.

PEANUT BUTTER COOKIES

NOT ILLUSTRATED

2 DOZEN

This classic cookie is as delicious as ever. If you like, add some chopped peanuts for extra crunch.

INGREDIENTS

◊ 1 cup all-purpose flour

◊ ½ tsp baking soda

◊ ½ tsp salt

◊ ½ cup (1 stick) unsalted butter, softened

◊ ¾ cup packed light brown sugar

◊ 1 egg, lightly beaten

◊ 1 tsp vanilla extract

◊ 1 cup crunchy peanut butter

◊ ½ cup peanuts, coarsely chopped

◊ Into a bowl, sift together flour, baking soda and salt. In a large bowl with electric mixer, beat butter until creamy, 30 seconds. Add sugar and continue beating, until mixture is light and fluffy, 1 to 2 minutes. Beat in egg and vanilla extract until well-blended. Beat in peanut butter and then, on low speed, beat in flour mixture and peanuts. Refrigerate dough until firm, about 30 minutes.

◊ Preheat oven to 350°F. Lightly grease 2 large baking sheets. Use a teaspoon to scoop out dough and form into 1-inch balls. Place on baking sheet 2 inches apart, and use a 4-tined fork to press flat, making 2½-inch rounds with a crisscross pattern.

◊ Bake until golden, 12 to 15 minutes. Remove baking sheets to wire racks to cool slightly. Then, using a metal pancake turner or palette knife, remove cookies to wire racks to cool completely. Store in airtight containers.

> **TIP**
> Smooth peanut butter can be used instead of crunchy. Be sure to use a commercial, not homemade, peanut butter.

MEXICAN WEDDING CAKES

LEFT & RIGHT

ABOUT 4 DOZEN

These melt-in-your-mouth cookies, dusted with several coats of confectioners' sugar, resemble wedding bells and are sometimes called by that name. They were probably originally made using walnuts, but I prefer the more refined flavor of pecans.

INGREDIENTS

◊ ¾ cup pecan or walnut halves

◊ ¾ cup confectioners' sugar

◊ ½ tsp ground cinnamon

◊ 1 cup (2 sticks) butter, cut into pieces, softened

◊ 1 tsp vanilla extract

◊ ¼ tsp salt

◊ 2 cups all-purpose flour

◊ confectioners' sugar for rolling

◊ Preheat oven to 375°F. Place pecans or walnuts on a baking sheet, and toast until golden and fragrant, 7 to 10 minutes, turning and shaking occasionally. Pour onto a plate to cool completely. Turn off oven.

◊ In a food processor fitted with metal blade, process toasted pecans or walnuts with confectioners' sugar and cinnamon until fine crumbs form. Add butter to processor, and process until creamy and smooth, scraping sides of bowl once. Add vanilla extract, and pulse to blend. Add salt and flour, and, using pulse action, process until mixture begins to stick together and form a soft dough. Scrape into a bowl, cover, and refrigerate 1 to 2 hours to firm.

◊ Preheat oven to 375°F. Using a small scoop or tablespoon and lightly floured hands, shape dough into 1-inch balls, rolling between your palms. Place balls 1½ inches apart on 2 large ungreased baking sheets. Bake until cookies are barely golden, 12 to 15 minutes, rotating baking sheets from top to bottom shelf and from front to back halfway through cooking time. Remove baking sheets to wire racks to cool, 2 minutes. Then, using a metal pancake turner or palette knife, remove cookies to wire racks. Repeat with remaining cookie dough.

◊ Place about 1 cup confectioners' sugar in a medium bowl. While cookies are still warm, roll a few at a time in sugar to coat well. Transfer to wire racks to cool completely. Roll again in confectioners' sugar before storing in airtight containers.

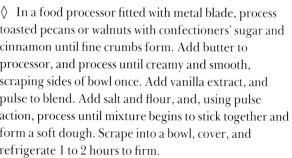

> **TIP**
> *I*f cookies have been stored, reroll in confectioners' sugar a few hours before serving, to insure they are well coated.

41

MOLDED COOKIES

CHINESE ALMOND COOKIES

ABOVE & RIGHT

ABOUT 2 DOZEN

These cookies are popular in Chinese restaurants and bakeries. They were originally made with bitter almonds and lard, but you can use half butter and lard or shortening or all butter.

◊ Into a medium bowl with electric mixer, beat butter or butter and shortening until creamy, 30 seconds. Add sugar and continue beating until light and fluffy, 1 to 2 minutes. Beat in eggs and almond extract until blended. On low speed, beat in flour mixture until soft dough forms. If dough is too soft to handle, refrigerate 10 to 15 minutes. Divide dough into 4 or 5 pieces.

◊ Preheat oven to 375°F. Lightly oil 2 large baking sheets. On a lightly floured surface, roll each piece of dough into a log shape 1 inch in diameter. Cut off 1-inch pieces and roll into small balls. Place balls on baking sheets, and using back of an oiled spoon, flatten slightly. Press an almond into center of each cookie.

◊ Bake cookies until lightly colored, 8 to 10 minutes. Remove baking sheets to wire racks to cool slightly. Then, using a metal pancake turner, remove cookies to wire racks to cool completely. Repeat with remaining dough and almonds. Store in airtight containers.

INGREDIENTS

◊ 3 cups cake or pastry flour

◊ ¾ tsp baking soda

◊ ½ tsp salt

◊ ⅔ cup (1 stick plus 2 tbsp) unsalted butter, softened or use ⅔ cup (1 stick) butter and 2 tbsp white vegetable shortening

◊ ½ cup sugar

◊ 2 eggs

◊ 1 tsp almond extract

◊ 1 egg yolk beaten with 1 tbsp water

◊ blanched almonds for decoration

POPPY SEED PISTACHIO PUFFS

NOT ILLUSTRATED

ABOUT 3 DOZEN

These tasty cookies are light as a feather. The flavors of poppy seed and pistachio go very well together.

INGREDIENTS

◊ 1½ cups all-purpose flour

◊ 6 tbsp poppy seeds

◊ ¼ tsp salt

◊ 1 cup (2 sticks) unsalted butter, softened

◊ ¾ cup superfine sugar

◊ 2 egg yolks

◊ grated zest from 2 oranges

◊ 1½ tsp vanilla extract

◊ 1 cup shelled fresh pistachios (or almonds)

◊ Into a bowl, combine flour, poppy seeds and salt. In a large bowl, beat butter until creamy, 30 to 60 seconds. Add sugar and continue beating until light and fluffy, 1 to 2 minutes. Beat in egg yolks, orange zest and vanilla extract. On low speed, gradually beat in flour mixture until soft dough forms. Scrape down sides of bowl and refrigerate, covered, until firm, about 1 hour.

◊ Preheat oven to 350°F. In a food processor fitted with metal blade, process pistachios (or almonds) until very fine. (Do not overprocess or paste will form.) Turn into a small bowl. Use a tablespoon to form dough into 1½-inch balls. Drop each ball, as it is formed, into nuts, and roll to coat well. Place the coated balls, 2 inches apart, on 2 large ungreased non-stick baking sheets.

◊ Bake until edges begin to brown, 18 to 20 minutes, rotating baking sheets from top to bottom shelf and front to back, halfway through cooking time. Remove baking sheets to wire racks to cool slightly. Then, using a thin metal palette knife, remove cookies to wire racks to cool completely. Store in airtight containers.

TRIPLE GINGER COOKIES

NOT ILLUSTRATED

ABOUT 3 DOZEN

These cookies are packed with ginger – ground, fresh and stem ginger – not for the faint-hearted!

INGREDIENTS

◊ 2¼ cups all-purpose flour

◊ 1 tbsp ground ginger

◊ 2 tbsp baking soda

◊ ½ tsp salt

◊ ¾ cup (1½ sticks) unsalted butter, softened

◊ 1 cup packed light or dark brown sugar

◊ ¼ cup molasses

◊ 1 egg

◊ 2 tbsp finely chopped fresh ginger root

◊ ½ cup stem ginger in syrup, drained and finely chopped, plus extra for decoration

◊ Into a medium bowl, sift together flour, ginger, baking soda and salt.

◊ In a large bowl with electric mixer, beat butter until creamy, 30 seconds. Add sugar and continue beating until light and fluffy, 1 to 2 minutes. Beat in molasses and egg until well-blended. Stir in flour mixture until blended; then stir in fresh ginger root and stem ginger.

◊ Form dough into ball and flatten to a disk shape; wrap tightly in plastic wrap and refrigerate 2 to 3 hours, or overnight, to chill completely.

◊ Preheat oven to 350°F. Lightly grease 2 large baking sheets. Use a tablespoon to scoop out mixture, and, using palms of your hands, form into 1½-inch balls. Place 2 inches apart on prepared baking sheets, and press a few pieces of stem ginger into center of each cookie. Bake until golden brown, about 10 minutes. Remove baking sheets to wire racks to cool slightly. Then remove cookies to wire racks to cool. Store in airtight containers.

> **TIP**
> *B*ottled stem ginger in syrup is available in gourmet and specialty stores, but crystallized ginger is an acceptable substitute.

GERMAN PEPPER NUTS

LEFT & ABOVE

ABOUT 40

These peppery, sugar-coated cookies are called *pfeffernüsse* in Germany, *pebernødder* in Denmark and *pepparnotter* in Sweden. They are popular all over northern Europe at Christmas.

INGREDIENTS

◊ 3½ cups all-purpose flour, plus extra if needed

◊ ¾ tsp baking soda

◊ ¾ tsp baking powder

◊ 1 tsp ground cinnamon

◊ ½ tsp ground white pepper

◊ ½ tsp ground ginger

◊ ¼ tsp ground cloves

◊ ¾ tsp salt

◊ 3 tbsp white vegetable shortening

◊ 1 cup honey

◊ 1 egg

◊ confectioners' sugar for dusting

◊ Into a large bowl, sift together flour, baking soda, baking powder, cinnamon, pepper, ginger, cloves and salt. Stir well to mix.

◊ In another large bowl, beat shortening until creamy, 1 minute. Gradually add honey and continue beating until well-blended, scraping the bowl occasionally. Beat in egg until well-mixed. With mixer on low speed, gradually beat in flour mixture until a soft dough forms, 2 to 3 minutes. Shape dough into a ball, and wrap tightly in plastic wrap, and refrigerate until firm.

◊ Preheat oven to 350°F. Lightly grease 2 large baking sheets. Soften dough slightly. Using a tablespoon, scoop out dough and with lightly floured hands, roll into 1-inch balls. Place balls 1 inch apart on baking sheets.

◊ Bake cookies until golden and slightly cracked, about 15 minutes, rotating baking sheets from top to bottom shelf and from front to back halfway through cooking time. Remove baking sheets to wire racks to cool slightly. Then remove cookies to wire racks to cool completely. Repeat with remaining dough.

◊ When cool, roll each cookie in confectioners' sugar to coat. Store in airtight containers.

CINNAMON BALLS

NOT ILLUSTRATED

ABOUT 20

These are a very popular Passover cookie, as they contain no flour.

INGREDIENTS

◊ 2 cups finely blanched and ground almonds, walnuts or pecans

◊ 1 cup superfine sugar

◊ 1 tbsp ground cinnamon

◊ 2 egg whites

◊ ⅛ tsp cream of tartar

◊ ½ cup confectioners' sugar

◊ 1 tbsp ground cinnamon

◊ Preheat oven to 325°F. Lightly grease a large non-stick baking sheet. In a medium bowl, combine ground nuts, ½ cup of the sugar and the cinnamon.

◊ In a medium bowl with electric mixer, beat egg whites until foamy. Add cream of tartar, and continue beating until soft peaks form. Gradually add remaining sugar, a tablespoon at a time, beating well after each addition, until whites are stiff and glossy. Gently fold in nut mixture.

◊ With moistened hands, shape mixture into walnut-size balls. Place on baking sheet 1 inch apart. Bake until set and golden, 25 to 30 minutes, rotating from top to bottom shelf and from front to back halfway through cooking time. Remove baking sheets to wire rack to cool slightly.

◊ In a small bowl, combine confectioners' sugar and cinnamon. Roll each warm cinnamon ball in mixture to coat completely; then set on wire rack to cool completely. Rolls balls again when cold. Store in airtight containers.

TIP
*I*f mixture is too soft, add a little more ground almond or fine matzo meal to stiffen it.

CHOCOLATE-DIPPED HAZELNUT CRESCENTS

ABOVE & RIGHT

ABOUT 36

The combination of chocolate and hazelnuts is beautiful, but the cookies are equally delicious on their own.

INGREDIENTS

◊ ⅔ cup hazelnuts

◊ 1 cup all-purpose flour

◊ 1 cup cake flour

◊ ¼ tsp salt

◊ 1 cup unsalted butter, softened

◊ ⅓ cup superfine sugar

◊ 1 tbsp hazelnut or almond-flavor liqueur, or water

◊ 1 tsp vanilla extract

◊ ½ cup grated or finely chopped chocolate

◊ confectioners' sugar for dusting

◊ 6 oz semisweet chocolate, melted, for dipping

◊ Preheat oven to 375°F. Place hazelnuts on a baking sheet, and toast until golden and fragrant, 5 to 7 minutes, turning and shaking frequently. Cool on a plate. Reduce oven temperature to 325°F. Into a medium bowl, sift together the flours and salt.

◊ In a food processor fitted with metal blade, process toasted hazelnuts until finely chopped but not ground; do not overprocess.

◊ In a large bowl with electric mixer, beat butter until creamy, about 1 minute. Add sugar and beat until mixture is light and fluffy, 1 to 2 minutes; beat in liqueur or water and vanilla extract. Gently stir in flour until just blended; then fold in chopped hazelnuts and grated or finely chopped chocolate.

◊ Using lightly floured hands, form dough into 1½-inch balls. Then roll balls into 2- × ½-inch crescent shapes, and place 2 inches apart on large ungreased baking sheet. Bake until edges are set and cookies are lightly golden, 20 to 25 minutes, rotating baking sheets from front to back halfway through cooking time. Remove baking sheet to wire rack to cool, 10 minutes. Then, using a metal pancake turner or palette knife, carefully remove each cookie to wire rack to cool completely. Repeat with remaining crescent shapes.

◊ Arrange crescents side by side on a wire rack over a baking sheet to catch drips; then dust with confectioners' sugar. Using kitchen tongs or fingers, dip half of each cookie into melted chocolate. Place on waxed paper-lined baking sheets, and refrigerate until set, 10 to 15 minutes. Store in airtight containers with waxed paper between the layers.

45

ALMOND AND PINE NUT BISCOTTI

ABOVE & BELOW

ABOUT 4 DOZEN

These dry nutty cookies are an Italian version of the German almond bread, *mandelbrot*. They are delicious with coffee or dunked in a glass of the sweet Italian wine, for dessert. They keep for a long time.

INGREDIENTS

◊ 3 cups all-purpose flour

◊ ½ cup finely ground almonds or fine semolina

◊ 1 tsp baking soda

◊ ½ tsp salt

◊ ½ tsp allspice

◊ 1 tsp cinnamon

◊ 1½ cups blanched almonds, toasted and coarsely chopped

◊ ¾ cup pine nuts, toasted

◊ 2 eggs, lightly beaten

◊ 1 cup superfine sugar

◊ ½ cup packed light brown sugar

◊ ¼ cup unsalted butter, melted and cooled

◊ 1½ tsp almond or vanilla extract

◊ grated zest of 1 lemon

◊ milk for glazing

◊ Preheat oven to 375°F. Line a large baking sheet with heavy-duty foil. In a large bowl, combine flour, ground almonds or semolina, baking soda, salt, allspice, cinnamon, chopped almonds and pine nuts. In another bowl, whisk eggs until foamy, then whisk in sugars, melted butter, almond or vanilla extract and lemon zest. Gradually stir flour mixture into egg mixture until a dough forms.

◊ Turn out onto a lightly floured surface, and knead gently just until nuts are evenly distributed in the dough. Divide dough into quarters, and form into even log-shapes about 10 inches by 3 inches long.

◊ Using a long metal palette knife, transfer each log, 2 to 3 inches apart, to prepared baking sheet. Brush each log lightly with a little milk, and bake until golden and a toothpick comes out clean when inserted in the center, 25 to 30 minutes, rotating baking sheet from front to back halfway through cooking time. Remove baking sheet to wire rack to cool, about 10 minutes. Reduce oven temperature to 325°F.

◊ While logs are still warm and soft, with a sharp knife, score logs crosswise into ½-inch wide slices. Slide foil onto work surface, and allow logs to cool until beginning to firm, about 10 minutes. Using a sharp serrated knife, cut through scored slices, and arrange, cut-sides down, on baking sheet (you may need another large baking sheet at this point). Bake biscotti under golden and crisp, 20 to 25 minutes, turning once halfway through cooking time.

◊ Remove biscotti to wire racks to cool completely. Allow to sit until crisp, 2 to 3 hours; then store in airtight containers or jars.

> **TIP**
> *These cookies are ideal to send to friends, as they store exceptionally well.*

GREEK CHRISTMAS WREATHS

ABOVE & BELOW

ABOUT 3 DOZEN

These rich sugar cookies are traditionally served at Christmas in Greece, but they are delicious anytime.

INGREDIENTS

◊ 3 cups all-purpose flour

◊ 1 tsp baking powder

◊ ½ tsp salt

◊ 1 cup (2 sticks) unsalted butter, softened

◊ ½ cup confectioners' sugar

◊ 1 extra large egg

◊ ¼ cup heavy cream

◊ 2 tbsp brandy or orange-flavor liqueur

GLAZE

◊ 1 egg yolk beaten with 1 tsp water

◊ ½ cup sesame seeds

◊ candied red cherries, chopped, to decorate

◊ Into a bowl, sift together flour, baking powder and salt; set aside. In a large bowl with electric mixer, beat butter until creamy, 1 minute. Add sugar and continue beating until light and fluffy, 1 to 2 minutes. Add egg, cream, brandy or orange-flavor liqueur, and continue beating until well-blended and creamy, 2 to 3 minutes.

◊ Gradually stir in the flour mixture until a soft dough forms. If dough is very sticky, sift over and stir in a little more flour, or chill 10 to 15 minutes for easier handling.

◊ With a teaspoon, scoop out dough, and, using floured hands, roll into walnut-size balls. On a lightly floured surface, roll into a rope about 16 inches long. Bend rope in half, and twist to form a coil; twist into a wreath shape, overlapping ends and pressing gently to secure.

◊ Arrange wreaths on 2 large greased baking sheets, 1 inch apart. Brush each wreath with a little egg glaze, and sprinkle with sesame seeds. Decorate with candied cherries, and bake until golden, about 20 minutes, rotating baking sheets from top to bottom shelf and from front to back halfway through cooking time.

◊ Remove baking sheets to wire racks to cool slightly. When firm, use a metal pancake turner or palette knife to remove cookies to wire racks to cool completely. Repeat with remaining cookie dough. Store in airtight containers with waxed paper between layers.

CHOCOLATE-NUT BISCOTTI

N O T   I L L U S T R A T E D

A B O U T   3   D O Z E N

In this recipe, the almonds of the classic German almond bread, *mandelbrot*, are replaced completely with hazelnuts.

INGREDIENTS

◊ 2 cups all-purpose flour

◊ 1½ tsp baking powder

◊ 1 tsp salt

◊ ¾ tsp ground cinnamon

◊ ½ tsp ground ginger

◊ ½ cup (1 stick) unsalted butter, softened

◊ 1¼ cups superfine sugar

◊ 2 eggs, lightly beaten

◊ grated zest of 1 orange

◊ ¼ cup freshly squeezed orange juice

◊ 1¾ cups hazelnuts, toasted, husked and coarsely chopped

◊ 1 cup semisweet chocolate chips or 6 oz semisweet chocolate, chopped

◊ 1 lb semisweet chocolate, melted

◊ In a large bowl, combine flour, baking powder, salt, cinnamon and ginger. In another large bowl with electric mixer, beat butter until creamy, 30 seconds. Add sugar and beat until light and fluffy, 1 to 2 minutes. On low speed, slowly add eggs, orange zest and juice and chopped nuts; increase speed to medium, and beat until well-blended. On low speed, gradually add flour mixture until a soft dough forms; then stir in chocolate.

◊ Divide dough in half. Lay 2 pieces of plastic wrap or foil on a work surface, and place one dough half on each piece. Using the wrap or foil as a guide, form each dough half into a log shape, about 3 inches in diameter. Wrap tightly and chill until firm, 20 to 30 minutes.

◊ Preheat oven to 375°F. Line a large baking sheet with heavy-duty foil. Place dough logs 3 to 4 inches apart on baking sheet, and flatten dough logs slightly to an oval shape. Bake until golden brown and tops begin to crack and toothpick inserted in center comes out clean, about 25 minutes, rotating baking sheet from front to back, halfway through cooking time. Remove baking sheet to wire rack to cool, about 10 minutes. Reduce oven to 325°F.

◊ While logs are still warm and soft, using a sharp knife, score them crosswise into ¼- to ½-inch wide slices. Slide foil onto work surface and allow logs to cool until beginning to firm, about 10 minutes. Using a sharp serrated knife, cut through scored slices, and arrange cut sides down on baking sheet. Bake biscotti until golden and crisp, 25 to 30 minutes, turning once halfway through. Remove baking sheets to wire rack to cool slightly. Then remove biscotti to wire racks to cool completely. Allow to sit, until crisp, 2 to 3 hours.

◊ Line a large baking sheet with waxed paper. Place melted chocolate in a medium bowl. Dip each biscotti halfway into chocolate, and place on waxed paper-lined baking sheets to set, 15 to 20 minutes.

SANDKAKERS

LEFT & RIGHT

ABOUT 4 DOZEN

These molded Swedish cookie-cakes are translated as "sand cakes," probably because the dough is as light and fine as sand; they are sometimes called sand tarts.

◊ 2 cups all-purpose flour

◊ ½ tsp salt

◊ 1 cup (2 sticks) unsalted butter, softened

◊ ¾ cup superfine sugar

◊ 1 tsp vanilla extract

◊ 1 egg, lightly beaten

◊ ⅓ cup chopped blanched almonds

◊ Preheat oven to 375°F. Generously butter as many sandkaker molds or tartlet pans as possible. Into a bowl, sift together the flour and salt; set aside.

◊ In a large bowl with electric mixer, beat butter until creamy, 30 seconds. Add sugar and vanilla extract, and beat until light and fluffy, 1 to 2 minutes. Add egg and beat until just mixed. On low speed, beat in flour and almonds until dough is smooth.

◊ Press about 2 teaspoons of dough into each mold or pan. For easier handling, place molds on a baking sheet. Bake until golden, 6 to 8 minutes. Remove baking sheet to wire rack to cool, 5 minutes. Then unmold cookies onto wire rack to cool completely. Repeat with remaining cookie dough. Store in airtight containers.

> **TIP**
> Sandkaker molds are available in specialty cookware shops, but I used miniature French tartlet pans. The more different shapes you have, the better.

SNICKERDOODLES

NOT ILLUSTRATED

ABOUT 4 DOZEN

This traditional New England cookie is made with flour, nuts and dried currants. As with other cookies from about this time, the name was made up and has no meaning.

INGREDIENTS

◊ 3½ cups all-purpose flour

◊ 1 tsp baking soda

◊ 1 tsp ground cinnamon

◊ ½ tsp ground nutmeg

◊ ½ cup (1 stick) unsalted butter, softened

◊ 1⅓ cups sugar

◊ 2 eggs

◊ ¼ cup milk

◊ 1 tsp vanilla extract

◊ ½ cup chopped walnuts or pecans

◊ ½ cup dried currants (optional)

COATING

◊ ½ cup sugar

◊ 2 tbsp ground cinnamon

◊ 1 tsp ground nutmeg

◊ Lightly grease 2 baking sheets. Into a large bowl, sift flour, baking soda and cinnamon; set aside.

◊ In a large bowl with electric mixer, beat butter until creamy, 30 seconds. Add sugar and continue beating until light and fluffy, 1 to 2 minutes. Beat in eggs, one at a time, beating well after each addition; then slowly beat in milk and vanilla extract until well-blended. Stir in flour until blended; then stir in chopped nuts. Refrigerate dough until just firm, 15 to 20 minutes.

◊ Preheat oven to 275°F. In a small bowl, stir together sugar and cinnamon. Roll dough into 1½-inch balls. Roll balls in sugar-cinnamon mixture, and place balls 2 inches apart on prepared baking sheets. Use fingertips to flatten slightly. Bake until golden, about 10 minutes. Remove baking sheets to wire racks to cool slightly. Then remove cookies to wire racks to cool.

COOKIE CANDY CANES

ABOVE, RIGHT & BELOW

2 DOZEN

This cookie dough can be shaped into candy canes or Christmas wreaths, then tinted whatever color you like.

INGREDIENTS

◊ 2½ cups all-purpose flour

◊ ¼ tsp salt

◊ 1 cup (2 sticks) unsalted butter, softened

◊ 1 cup confectioners' sugar, sifted

◊ 1 egg

◊ ½ tsp vanilla extract

◊ ½ tsp peppermint extract

◊ ¼ tsp red food coloring, optional

◊ ¼ cup crushed peppermint candy

◊ Into a bowl, sift flour and salt. In a large bowl, beat butter until creamy, 30 seconds. Gradually add sugar and beat until light and fluffy, 1 to 2 minutes. Beat in egg, and vanilla and peppermint extracts until blended. On low speed, gradually beat in flour.

◊ Remove half the dough to a piece of plastic wrap, and wrap tightly. Add food coloring and crushed peppermint candy to remaining dough, and beat until completely mixed. Wrap tightly in plastic wrap, and refrigerate doughs until firm, about 1 hour.

◊ Preheat oven to 350°F. Line 2 large baking sheets with foil or non-stick baking parchment. To form cookies, use a teaspoon to scoop out a piece of plain dough; then roll into a log shape, 4 inches long. Repeat with red-colored dough; then twist the logs together, and bend top end to form into a cane shape. Set canes 2 inches apart on lined baking sheets.

◊ Bake until firm, 8 to 10 minutes; do not allow to brown. Remove baking sheets to wire racks to cool slightly. Then remove cookies to wire tray to cool.

> **TIP**
> *I*f you like, tie a red ribbon around top of candy cane to use as a Christmas tree decoration.

RICH CARDAMOM COOKIES

RIGHT & BELOW

ABOUT 2 DOZEN

These rich butter cookies are flavored with cardamom, a favorite Scandinavian spice.

INGREDIENTS

◊ 2 cups cake flour

◊ 4 tsp ground cardamom

◊ ¼ tsp salt

◊ ¾ cup (1½ sticks) unsalted butter, softened

◊ ½ cup superfine sugar

◊ ½ cup sliced or flaked almonds

TO DECORATE

◊ ⅓ cup confectioners' sugar

◊ 1½ tsp cardamom

◊ sliced or flaked almonds

◊ Preheat oven to 375°F. Grease 2 large baking sheets. Into a medium bowl, sift together flour, cardamom and salt.

◊ In a large bowl with electric mixer, beat butter until creamy, 30 seconds. Gradually add sugar and continue beating until light and fluffy, 1 to 2 minutes. On low speed, gradually beat in flour mixture until well-blended; then stir in sliced or flaked almonds.

◊ Into a small bowl, sift together confectioners' sugar and cardamom. Using a tablespoon, scoop out dough and roll into 1½-inch balls. Drop balls one at a time into sugar-spice mixture, rolling to coat well. Place 1½ inches apart on baking sheets. Dip bottom of a glass into sugar mixture, and flatten cookies to ½-inch thick rounds. Press 2 or 3 sliced or flaked almonds onto tops of cookies.

◊ Bake cookies until golden brown, 12 to 14 minutes, rotating baking sheets from top to bottom shelf and from front to back halfway through cooking time. Remove baking sheets to wire racks to cool, 2 to 3 minutes. Then, using a thin metal palette knife, remove cookies to wire racks to cool completely. Store in airtight containers.

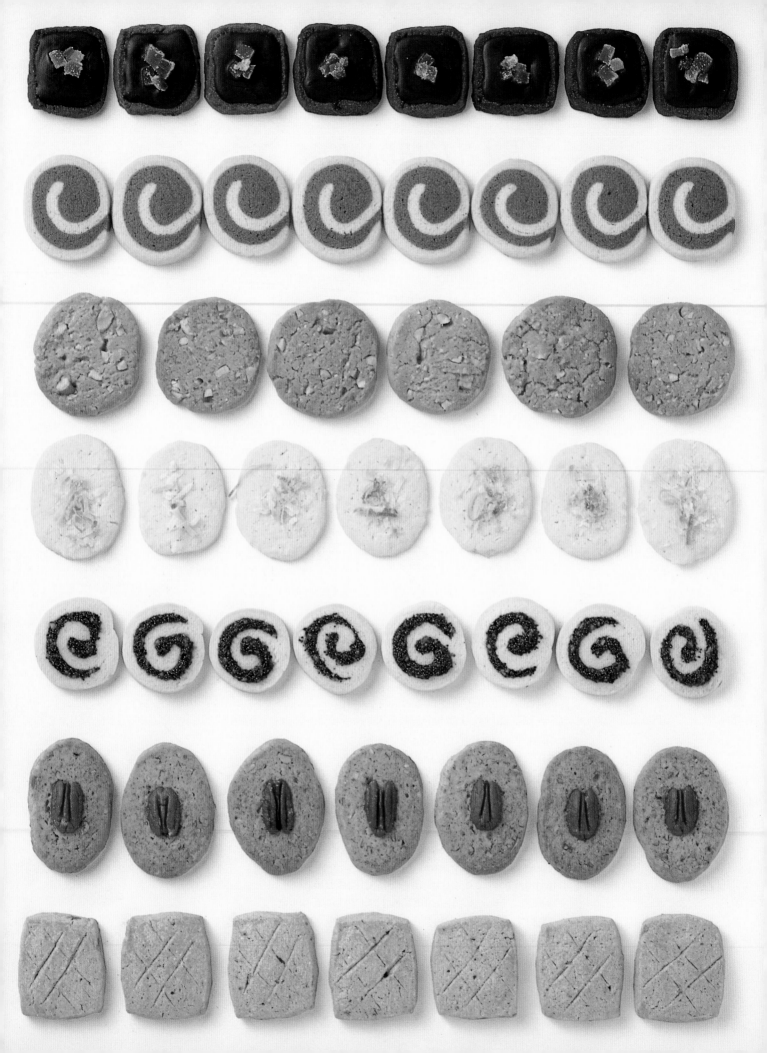

3

REFRIGERATOR
Cookies

Made using a stiff dough, these

cookies can be stored in the refrigerator for several

days, or frozen for up to six months.

HAZELNUT-ORANGE WHIRLS

LEFT & ABOVE

ABOUT **4** DOZEN

These two-tone cookies can be made with walnuts or pecans, but the hazelnuts go well with the orange.

INGREDIENTS

◊ 1 cup hazelnuts, toasted and finely ground

◊ ½ cup orange marmalade

◊ ⅓ cup raisins, finely chopped

◊ ½ tsp ground cinnamon

◊ zest of 1 grated orange

◊ 1 cup plus 3 tbsp packed light brown sugar

◊ ¼ cup butter or margarine

◊ ¼ cup white vegetable shortening

◊ 1¾ cups all-purpose flour

◊ 1 egg

◊ In a bowl, combine hazelnuts, marmalade, raisins, cinnamon, orange zest and 3 tablespoons brown sugar.

◊ In a medium bowl with electric mixer, beat butter or margarine, shortening, flour and egg until a stiff dough forms. Divide the dough in half.

◊ On a piece of plastic wrap or waxed paper, roll out one piece of dough to a 6- by 14-inch rectangle and spread with half the nut mixture. Starting at one short side, roll up dough jelly-roll fashion and wrap tightly. Repeat with remaining dough and nut mixture. Refrigerate dough several hours or overnight until firm. (Dough can be refrigerated up to 5 days or frozen.)

◊ Preheat oven to 350°F. Lightly grease 2 large baking sheets. Cut one dough roll crosswise into ¼-inch slices, and place 1 inch apart on prepared baking sheets. Bake until golden, about 10 minutes. Remove baking sheets to wire rack to cool slightly. Then, using a metal pancake turner, remove cookies to wire racks to cool completely. Repeat with remaining dough roll. Store in airtight containers.

OATMEAL COCONUT CRUNCHIES

NOT ILLUSTRATED

ABOUT 2 DOZEN

These crisp cookies contain no flour and use old-fashioned oats for real texture.

INGREDIENTS

◊ ⅔ cup unsalted butter, softened

◊ ½ cup superfine sugar

◊ 2 cups old-fashioned oats

◊ 1 cup shredded coconut

◊ ½ tsp ground cinnamon

◊ ¼ tsp ground ginger

◊ ¼ tsp ground nutmeg

◊ 1 tsp vanilla extract

◊ grated zest of 1 lemon

◊ grated zest of 1 orange

◊ ¼ tsp salt

◊ In a large bowl, beat butter and sugar until light and fluffy, 1 to 2 minutes. Stir in remaining ingredients until well-blended.

◊ Scrape dough onto a piece of plastic wrap or waxed paper, and, using wrap or paper as a guide, form into a roll 1 inch in diameter. Refrigerate several hours or overnight until very firm. (Dough can be made up to 5 days ahead or frozen.)

◊ Preheat oven to 325°F. Using a sharp knife, cut dough log crosswise into ¼-inch slices, and place 1 inch apart on 2 large ungreased baking sheets. Bake until golden, 15 to 17 minutes, rotating baking sheets from top to bottom shelf and from front to back halfway through cooking time. Remove baking sheets to wire racks to cool slightly. Then, using a metal pancake turner or palette knife, remove cookies to wire racks to cool completely. Store in airtight containers with waxed paper between layers.

CHEDDAR PENNIES

RIGHT & BOTTOM LEFT

ABOUT 4 DOZEN

Although not a sweet cookie, these spicy cheese rounds are so popular (in America) I had to include them. They are usually served with a drink and make a change from peanuts and chips.

INGREDIENTS

◊ ½ cup (1 stick) unsalted butter, softened

◊ 1 cup grated medium or sharp Cheddar cheese

◊ 1 cup all-purpose flour

◊ 3 tbsp fresh chopped chives

◊ ⅛ tsp salt

◊ ¼ to ½ tsp cayenne pepper or chili powder

◊ In a large bowl with electric mixer, beat butter until creamy, 30 seconds. Stir in grated cheese, flour, chives, salt and cayenne pepper or chili powder to form a soft dough.

◊ Scrape onto a piece of plastic wrap or waxed paper and using wrap or paper as a guide, form into a long log about 1½-inches in diameter (for smaller pennies, form dough into a 1-inch log). Wrap tightly, and refrigerate several hours or overnight until firm. (Dough can be made up to 5 days ahead or frozen.)

◊ Preheat oven to 350°F. Lightly grease 2 large baking sheets. Using a sharp knife, cut dough log (or logs) into ⅜-inch slices and place on prepared baking sheets. Bake until slightly puffed and golden, 10 to 12 minutes. Using a metal pancake turner or palette knife, remove cookies to a wire rack to cool. Store in airtight containers.

> **TIP**
>
> This is a good way to use up small pieces of hard cheese, such as Cheddar or Monterey Jack, but the cheese should be well flavored and not bland or the pennies won't have a good flavor.

LEMON WAFERS

NOT ILLUSTRATED

ABOUT 50

These thin, delicate cookies have a lovely lemon flavor. They are perfect to serve with fruit sorbets.

INGREDIENTS

◊ 1½ cups all-purpose flour

◊ ½ tsp baking powder

◊ ½ tsp baking soda

◊ ¼ tsp salt

◊ ½ cup white vegetable shortening, softened

◊ 2 tbsp unsalted butter, softened

◊ 1 cup superfine sugar

◊ ½ tsp vanilla extract

◊ ¾ tsp lemon extract

◊ grated zest and juice of 1 lemon

◊ confectioners' sugar for dusting

◊ Into a medium bowl, sift together the flour, baking powder, baking soda and salt; set aside.

◊ In a large bowl with electric mixer, beat shortening and butter until creamy, 30 to 60 seconds. Gradually add sugar and continue beating until light and fluffy, 1 to 2 minutes. Beat in vanilla and lemon extracts, and grated lemon zest and juice. Stir in flour until soft dough forms.

◊ Scrape dough onto a piece of plastic wrap or waxed paper, and, using wrap or paper as a guide, form dough into a log about 1½ inches in diameter. Wrap tightly, and refrigerate several hours or overnight until very firm. (Dough can be made up to 5 days ahead or frozen.)

◊ Preheat oven to 350°F. Slice log crosswise into ⅛-inch slices, or as thin as possible, and place dough rounds 2 inches apart on 2 large non-stick baking sheets. Bake until golden around edges but still pale in center, about 8 minutes. Remove baking sheets to wire racks to cool slightly. Then, using a metal pancake turner or palette knife, remove cookies to wire racks to cool completely. Before serving dust cookies with confectioners' sugar. Store in airtight containers.

> **TIP**
> Do not allow cookies to cool on baking sheets or they will be too crisp to remove.

POPPY SEED SWIRLS

ABOVE & BELOW

ABOUT 4 DOZEN

Poppy seeds form the basis of the filling in these crisp cookie swirls.

INGREDIENTS

◊ ½ cup walnut pieces, finely ground

◊ ½ cup poppy seeds

◊ ⅓ cup honey

◊ ½ tsp ground cinnamon

◊ grated zest of 1 orange

◊ 6 tbsp unsalted butter, softened

◊ ½ cup superfine sugar

◊ 1 egg, lightly beaten

◊ 1 tsp vanilla extract

◊ 1½ cups all-purpose flour

◊ In a small bowl, combine walnuts, poppy seeds, honey, cinnamon, orange zest and 2 tablespoons of the softened butter until mixture forms a paste. Set aside.

◊ In a large bowl with electric mixer, beat remaining butter and sugar until light and fluffy, 1 to 2 minutes. Beat in egg and vanilla extract until well-blended, then slowly beat in flour until a soft dough forms. Refrigerate dough until firm enough to handle, 15 to 20 minutes.

◊ On a lightly floured sheet of waxed paper or non-stick baking parchment, roll out dough to a 6- by 12-inch rectangle and spread with poppy seed paste. Starting at one short side, roll up dough jelly-roll fashion and wrap tightly. Refrigerate several hours or overnight until firm. (Dough can be refrigerated up to 5 days or frozen.)

◊ Preheat oven to 375°F. Lightly grease 2 large non-stick baking sheets. Slice dough roll crosswise into ¼-inch slices and place ½ inch apart on baking sheets. Bake until golden, about 10 minutes. Remove baking sheets to wire racks to cool slightly. Then, using a metal pancake turner or palette knife, remove cookies to wire racks to cool completely. Repeat with remaining slices. Store in airtight containers.

CASHEW BUTTER ROUNDS

LEFT & BELOW

ABOUT 4 ½ DOZEN

These delicious cookies are enriched by the "cashew butter." A food processor is necessary to make the cashew butter, although it can be bought at some health food stores.

INGREDIENTS

◊ 1 cup unsalted roasted cashews

◊ 2 tbsp vegetable oil

◊ 1⅔ cups all-purpose flour

◊ 1 tsp baking soda

◊ ½ tsp salt

◊ ½ cup (1 stick) unsalted butter, softened

◊ ½ cup sugar

◊ ½ cup packed light or dark brown sugar

◊ 1 egg

◊ 2 tbsp rum or brandy

◊ 1 tsp vanilla extract

◊ 1 cup chopped roasted cashews

◊ ½ cup old-fashioned oats

◊ In a food processor fitted with metal blade, process cashews and oil until a thick, smooth paste forms, just like peanut butter. Into a medium bowl, sift together flour, baking soda and salt; set aside.

◊ In a large bowl with electric mixer, beat butter until creamy, 30 seconds. Add sugars and beat until light and fluffy, 1 to 2 minutes. Beat in egg, cashew butter, rum or brandy and vanilla extract until well-blended.

◊ On low speed, gradually beat in flour mixture until a soft dough is formed. Stir in chopped nuts and oats. On a lightly floured surface, form dough into two 2-inch logs. Wrap each log tightly in plastic wrap, and refrigerate 4 to 6 hours, or overnight until very firm.

◊ Preheat oven to 350°F. Lightly grease 2 large baking sheets. Cut dough log crosswise into ⅜-inch slices, and place slices 1 inch apart on baking sheets. Bake until golden, 10 to 12 minutes. Remove baking sheets to wire racks to cool slightly. Then, using a metal pancake turner or palette knife, remove to wire racks to cool completely. Repeat with remaining dough as cookies are required. Store in airtight containers.

> **TIP**
> Cookie dough can be refrigerated up to 5 days or frozen. Defrost overnight in refrigerator before using. Cut off as many slices as you require for baking at one time.

Belgian Almond Cookies

LEFT & RIGHT

ABOUT **3** DOZEN

This is a traditional cookie found in Belgium. I've rolled the dough log in chopped almonds for a prettier effect.

INGREDIENTS

◊ 3 tbsp unsalted butter

◊ ¼ cup milk

◊ 2 tbsp brandy

◊ 2 cups all-purpose flour

◊ ½ tsp baking powder

◊ ¾ tsp ground cinnamon

◊ ¼ tsp salt

◊ 1 cup grated or very finely chopped blanched almonds

◊ ½ cup packed light brown sugar

◊ 1 cup chopped blanched almonds

◊ In a small saucepan over low heat, melt butter. Remove from heat and cool slightly. Stir in milk and brandy; set aside.

◊ Into a large bowl, sift together flour, baking powder, cinnamon and salt. Stir in grated or finely chopped almonds and sugar. Stir in butter mixture to form a soft dough. (If dough is too soft, add a little more flour.)

◊ Scrape dough onto a piece of plastic wrap or waxed paper, and using wrap or paper as a guide, form dough into 2-inch roll. Chill dough 5 to 10 minutes. Sprinkle chopped blanched almonds on a work surface, and roll dough log in almonds to coat, pressing almonds into surface. Rewrap log, and refrigerate several hours or overnight until firm.

◊ Preheat oven to 375°F. Lightly grease 2 large baking sheets. Cut log crosswise into ½-inch slices, and place 1 inch apart on prepared baking sheets. Bake until golden, about 10 minutes. Remove baking sheets to wire rack to cool slightly. Then, using a metal pancake turner or palette knife, remove cookies to wire racks to cool completely. Store in airtight containers.

CHOCOLATE-GINGER FREEZER COOKIES

LEFT & RIGHT

ABOUT 3 DOZEN

The combination of chocolate and ginger is a
wonderful one. These cookies use fresh ginger
root and have a definite zing!

◊ 2- to 3-inch piece of fresh
ginger root

◊ 1½ cups all-purpose flour

◊ 2 tbsp unsweetened cocoa
powder (preferably Dutch-
processed)

◊ 1 cup whole wheat flour

◊ ½ tsp salt

◊ ¼ tsp finely ground black
pepper

◊ 1 cup (2 sticks) unsalted
butter, softened

◊ 1 cup packed dark brown
sugar

◊ 2 egg yolks

◊ 2 tsp vanilla extract

◊ 12 oz bittersweet or
semisweet chocolate, chopped
crystallized ginger to decorate

◊ Using the small round holes of a box grater, grate
ginger root; set aside. Into a medium bowl, sift together
all-purpose flour and cocoa powder. Stir in whole wheat
flour, salt and pepper.

◊ In a large bowl with electric mixer, beat butter until
creamy, 30 seconds. Add brown sugar and continue
beating until light and fluffy, 1 to 2 minutes. Beat in egg
yolks, vanilla extract and grated ginger root until
mixture is smooth and well-blended. Stir in flour
mixture until blended.

◊ Scrape out onto a piece of plastic wrap, and, using
wrap as a guide, shape dough into a 3-inch log. Wrap
tightly and freeze until hard. (Dough can be frozen up
to 2 months.)

◊ Preheat oven to 350°F. Line 2 large baking sheets
with non-stick baking parchment. Using a sharp knife,
cut frozen dough log into ¼-inch slices, and place 1 inch
apart on baking sheets.

◊ Bake until lightly colored, about 15 minutes, rotating
baking sheets from top to bottom shelf and from front
to back halfway through cooking time. Remove baking
sheets to wire rack to cool, about 1 minute. Then, using
a metal pancake turner or palette knife, carefully
remove each cookie to wire racks to cool completely.

◊ Place chopped chocolate in a bowl over a pan of
simmering water. Stir until melted and smooth. Remove
chocolate from heat, and set aside to cool, stirring
occasionally. When chocolate reaches a spreading
consistency, use a small palette knife to spread a little on
each cookie. Top each cookie with a piece of crystallized
ginger, and allow cookies to set. Store cookies in airtight
containers with waxed paper between layers.

TIP
A food processor
is ideal for
grating or
puréeing the fresh
ginger root.

Chocolate and Vanilla Pinwheels

LEFT & RIGHT

ABOUT 5 DOZEN

Be careful not to overbake these pretty pinwheels
or the color contrast could be lost.

INGREDIENTS

◊ 3 cups all-purpose flour

◊ ½ tsp salt

◊ 1 cup (2 sticks) unsalted butter, softened

◊ 1 cup superfine sugar

◊ 2 eggs, lightly beaten

◊ 2 tsp vanilla extract

◊ 1 oz unsweetened chocolate, melted and cooled

◊ Into a medium bowl, sift together flour and salt. In a large bowl with electric mixer, beat butter until creamy, 30 to 60 seconds. Add sugar and continue beating until light and fluffy, 1 to 2 minutes. Beat in eggs and vanilla extract until blended. On low speed, beat in flour until well-blended.

◊ Divide dough in half, and wrap one half in plastic wrap; refrigerate until firm enough to roll. Add melted chocolate to remaining dough in bowl, and mix until completely blended. Wrap chocolate dough in plastic wrap, and refrigerate until firm enough to roll.

◊ On a lightly floured surface or between 2 sheets of plastic wrap or waxed paper, roll half the vanilla dough to a ¼-inch thick, 4-inch wide rectangle. Repeat with half the chocolate dough, rolling to the same size.

◊ If rolling between sheets of waxed paper, remove top sheet and turn chocolate dough over onto vanilla dough; roll lightly to seal. Roll up dough, jelly-roll fashion, as tightly as possible. Wrap tightly in plastic wrap, and repeat with remaining doughs. Refrigerate dough rolls several hours or overnight until firm. (Dough can be prepared ahead up to 5 days or frozen.)

◊ Preheat oven to 375°F. Lightly grease 2 large baking sheets. Using a sharp knife, cut dough rolls into ¼-inch slices, and place 1 inch apart on prepared baking sheets. Bake until just beginning to color, 7 to 10 minutes. Using a metal pancake turner or palette knife, remove cookies to wire racks to cool.

> **TIP**
>
> *T*o make Lemon or Orange Chocolate Pinwheels, reduce vanilla extract to 1 teaspoon, and add 2 to 3 teaspoons grated lemon or orange zest to "white" dough half before chilling dough.

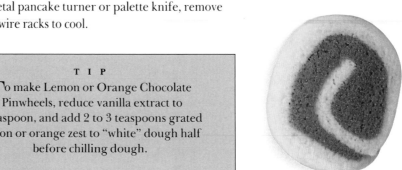

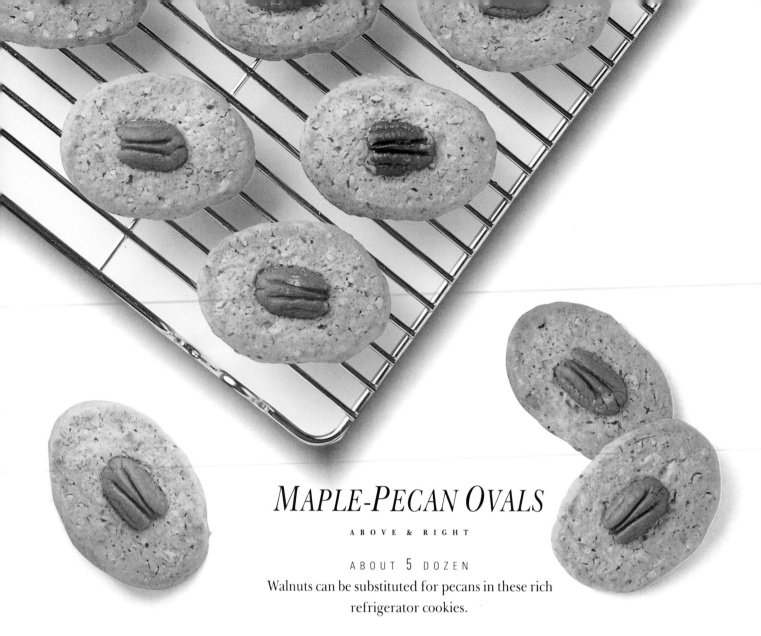

MAPLE-PECAN OVALS

ABOVE & RIGHT

ABOUT 5 DOZEN

Walnuts can be substituted for pecans in these rich refrigerator cookies.

INGREDIENTS

◊ 2 cups all-purpose flour

◊ ¼ tsp baking soda

◊ ¼ tsp salt

◊ 2 cups (2 sticks) unsalted butter, softened

◊ ½ cup sugar

◊ ¼ cup packed light brown sugar

◊ 1 egg

◊ ¾ tsp natural maple extract

◊ 1 cup finely chopped pecans

◊ ¾ cup finely chopped dates

◊ pecan halves for decoration

◊ Into a medium bowl, sift together flour, baking soda and salt. In a large bowl with electric mixer, beat butter until creamy, 30 seconds. Add sugars and continue beating until light and fluffy, 1 to 2 minutes. Beat in egg and maple extract. On low speed, add flour until just combined. Then stir in chopped nuts and dates.

◊ Divide dough in half, and form into two 9-inch logs. Flatten slightly to form 2 oval logs. Wrap tightly in plastic wrap, and refrigerate overnight or until firm. (Dough can be refrigerated up to 5 days or frozen.)

◊ Preheat oven to 350°F. Lightly grease 2 large baking sheets. Slice one dough oval crosswise into ¼-inch ovals, and place 1 inch apart on prepared baking sheets. Press a pecan half into center of each oval.

◊ Bake until golden, about 12 minutes. Remove baking sheets to wire racks to cool slightly. Then, using a metal pancake turner or palette knife, remove cookies to wire rack to cool completely. Repeat with remaining dough oval and pecan halves. Store in airtight containers.

PEANUT ROUNDS

ABOUT 5 DOZEN

These cookies have a wonderfully fresh peanut flavor, enhanced by drizzled chocolate.

INGREDIENTS

◊ ¾ cup unsalted peanuts

◊ 2 cups all-purpose flour

◊ ½ tsp salt

◊ ¼ tsp baking powder

◊ 1 cup (2 sticks) unsalted butter, softened

◊ ¾ cup packed light brown sugar

◊ 1 egg

◊ 1 tsp vanilla extract

◊ peanuts to decorate

◊ 4 oz milk or semisweet chocolate, melted for drizzling (optional)

◊ In a food processor fitted with metal blade, process peanuts until a smooth paste forms, set aside. Into a medium bowl, sift together flour, salt and baking powder.

◊ In a large bowl, beat butter until creamy, 30 seconds. Add sugar and continue beating until light and fluffy, 1 to 2 minutes. Beat in egg and vanilla extract until well-blended. On low speed, beat in the ground peanut mixture and flour until soft dough forms.

◊ Divide dough in half and form into 2 8-inch logs. Wrap tightly in plastic wrap, and refrigerate overnight or until firm. (Dough can be refrigerated up to 5 days or frozen.)

◊ Preheat oven to 350°F. Lightly grease 2 large baking sheets. Slice one dough log into ¼-inch slices, and place ½ inch apart on baking sheets. Press a whole peanut into center of each round.

◊ Bake cookies until golden, 8 to 10 minutes. Remove baking sheets to wire racks to cool slightly. Then, using a metal pancake turner or palette knife, remove cookies to wire racks to cool completely. Repeat with remaining dough log and peanuts.

◊ Arrange cookies close together on wire racks. Spoon melted chocolate into a paper cone (page 14), and drizzle chocolate over cookies. Allow chocolate to set. Store in airtight containers with waxed paper between layers.

ALMOND CRISPS

ABOUT 36

This crisp cookie uses ground almonds entirely instead of flour. For the best flavor grind the almonds yourself; bought ground almonds are not as flavorsome.

INGREDIENTS

◊ 1½ cups blanched almonds, toasted

◊ ⅓ cup superfine sugar

◊ ½ cup (1 stick) unsalted butter, softened

◊ ¼ tsp salt

◊ ½ tsp vanilla extract

◊ ½ tsp almond extract

◊ confectioners' sugar for dusting (optional)

◊ In a food processor fitted with metal blade, process toasted almonds with 1 tablespoon of the sugar until finely ground. Do not overprocess or a paste may form.

◊ In a medium bowl, beat butter and remaining sugar until light and fluffy, 1 to 2 minutes. Beat in salt and vanilla and almond extracts. Stir in ground almond mixture until a soft dough forms.

◊ Scrape dough onto a piece of plastic wrap or waxed paper and, using wrap or paper as a guide, form dough into a roll 1 inch in diameter. Refrigerate several hours or overnight until very firm. (Dough can be made up to 5 days ahead or frozen.)

◊ Preheat oven to 350°F. Using a sharp knife, cut dough log crosswise into ⅛-inch slices and place 1 inch apart on 2 large ungreased baking sheets. Bake until just golden, about 5 minutes. Remove baking sheets to wire racks to cool slightly. Then, using a metal pancake turner or palette knife, remove cookies to wire racks to cool completely. Store in airtight containers. If you like, dust with confectioners' sugar before serving.

> **TIP**
>
> This cookie can be made with walnuts or pecans. Be careful not to overprocess when chopping the nuts.

CINNAMON DIAMOND COOKIES

L E F T & R I G H T

ABOUT 5 DOZEN

These refrigerator cookies are sweet and crisp –
just the thing to serve with ice cream.

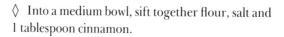

INGREDIENTS

◊ 2¼ cups all-purpose flour

◊ ½ tsp salt

◊ 1 tbsp ground cinnamon

◊ 1 cup (2 sticks) unsalted butter, softened

◊ ¾ cup packed light brown sugar

◊ 2 eggs, lightly beaten

◊ 1 tsp vanilla extract

◊ ½ cup superfine sugar for sprinkling

◊ 1 tsp ground cinnamon

◊ 1 egg yolk beaten with 2 tbsp water for glazing

◊ Into a medium bowl, sift together flour, salt and 1 tablespoon cinnamon.

◊ In a large bowl with electric mixer, beat butter until creamy, 30 seconds. Add brown sugar and continue beating until light and fluffy, 1 to 2 minutes. Gradually beat in eggs and vanilla extract until well-blended. Stir in flour mixture.

◊ Divide dough in half, and scrape onto a piece of plastic wrap or waxed paper. Using wrap or paper as a guide, form each dough half into a log about 2 inches in diameter; flatten log on 4 sides to form a rectangular shape. Wrap tightly, and refrigerate several hours or overnight until firm. (Dough can be made ahead up to 5 days or frozen.)

◊ Preheat oven to 375°F. Lightly grease 2 large baking sheets. In a small bowl, combine superfine sugar and 1 teaspoon cinnamon. With a sharp knife, cut the log into ¼-inch squares and place 1 inch apart on prepared baking sheets. Brush each square with a little egg yolk; then, using a sharp knife, score each to make a diamond pattern, and sprinkle with a little sugar-cinnamon mixture. Bake until golden, about 10 minutes. Remove baking sheets to wire racks to cool slightly. Then, using a metal pancake turner or palette knife, remove cookies to wire racks to cool completely. Repeat with remaining cookie dough and sugar mixture. Store in airtight containers.

Chocolate Nut Disks

NOT ILLUSTRATED

ABOUT 5 DOZEN

These cookies are sweet and crisp with a chocolate flavor and nutty crunch.

INGREDIENTS

◊ 1 oz semisweet chocolate, chopped

◊ 1 oz unsweetened chocolate, chopped

◊ 2 cups all-purpose flour

◊ ½ tsp salt

◊ 1 cup (2 sticks) unsalted butter, softened

◊ 1 cup superfine sugar

◊ 2 eggs, lightly beaten

◊ 1 tsp vanilla extract

◊ 1 cup pecans, walnuts or hazelnuts, finely chopped

◊ In a small heat-proof bowl over saucepan of simmering water over low heat, melt chocolates until smooth, stirring frequently. Remove from heat, and set aside to cool. Into a medium bowl, sift together flour and salt.

◊ In a large bowl with electric mixer, beat butter until creamy, 30 seconds. Add sugar and continue beating until light and fluffy, 1 to 2 minutes. Beat in eggs and vanilla extract until well-blended. Gradually beat in melted chocolate; then stir in flour and chopped nuts.

◊ Divide dough in half, and scrape each piece of dough onto a piece of plastic wrap or waxed paper. Using wrap or paper as guide, form each dough half into a log about 2-inches in diameter. Wrap tightly, and refrigerate several hours, overnight, or until firm. (Dough can be made ahead up to 5 days or frozen.)

◊ Preheat oven to 375°F. Lightly grease 2 large baking sheets. With a sharp knife, cut log into ¼-inch slices, and place 1 inch apart on prepared sheets. Bake until golden, about 10 minutes. Remove baking sheets to wire racks to cool slightly. Then, using a metal pancake turner or palette knife, remove cookies to wire racks to cool completely. Repeat with remaining cookie dough. Store in airtight containers.

Coconut Crisps

RIGHT & BELOW

ABOUT 5 DOZEN

These cookies have a lovely flavor. If you like, add a few chopped raisins.

INGREDIENTS

◊ 2 cups plus 2 tbsp all-purpose flour

◊ ½ tsp salt

◊ 1 cup (2 sticks) unsalted butter, softened

◊ 1 cup sugar

◊ 2 eggs, lightly beaten

◊ ½ tsp vanilla extract

◊ ½ tsp almond extract

◊ ¾ cup shredded coconut

◊ toasted coconut for garnish

◊ Into a medium bowl, sift together flour and salt. In a large bowl, beat butter until creamy, 30 seconds. Add sugar and continue beating until light and fluffy, 1 to 2 minutes. Beat in eggs and vanilla and almond extracts until well-blended. Stir in flour and shredded coconut.

◊ Divide dough in half, and scrape onto 2 pieces of plastic wrap or waxed paper. Using wrap or paper as a guide, form each dough half into a log about 2 inches in diameter. Wrap tightly, and refrigerate several hours or overnight until firm. (Dough can be made up to 5 days ahead or frozen.)

◊ Preheat oven to 375°F. Lightly grease 2 large baking sheets. Using a sharp knife, cut one dough log into ¼-inch slices and place 1 inch apart on prepared baking sheets and sprinkle cookies with a little toasted coconut. Bake until just golden, about 10 minutes. Remove baking sheets to wire racks to cool slightly. Then, using a metal pancake turner or palette knife, remove cookies to wire racks to cool completely. Repeat with remaining dough log. Store in airtight containers.

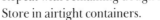

4

ROLLED Cookies

The cookie dough is rolled flat

and cut with shaped cutters. The range

of fun shapes available today is tremendous.

MORAVIAN SPICE SQUARES

ABOVE & BELOW

ABOUT 2 ½ DOZEN

The Moravians were a sect of German settlers, known as the Pennsylvania Dutch, whose baked goods often included molasses and spices such as ginger, cinnamon and cloves.

INGREDIENTS

◊ ¼ cup (½ stick) unsalted butter

◊ ¼ cup packed dark brown sugar

◊ 2 tbsp molasses

◊ 1¼ cups all-purpose flour

◊ grated zest of 1 lemon

◊ 1 tsp ground ginger

◊ 1 tsp ground cinnamon

◊ ½ tsp baking soda

◊ ¼ tsp ground cloves

◊ sugar for sprinkling

◊ In a medium saucepan over medium heat, cook butter, brown sugar and molasses until melted and smooth, stirring often. Remove from heat, and stir in flour, lemon zest, ginger, cinnamon, baking soda and cloves until well-blended.

◊ Scrape dough onto a piece of waxed paper or plastic wrap, and, using paper or wrap as a guide, shape into a flat disk. Wrap tightly and refrigerate several hours or overnight. (Dough can be made up to 5 days ahead.)

◊ Preheat oven to 350°F. Lightly grease 2 large baking sheets. On a lightly floured surface, using a floured rolling pin, roll one half of the dough into a 10- by 10-inch square. Using a sharp knife or pastry wheel, cut dough into 1½-inch squares, and place about 1 inch apart on prepared baking sheet.

◊ With fork, gently prick cookie squares to prevent pastry puffing, and sprinkle each with sugar. Bake until just set, about 7 minutes. With a palette knife, remove cookies to wire racks to cool completely. Repeat with remaining dough. Store in airtight containers.

VIENNESE POCKETS

RIGHT

ABOUT 3 ½ DOZEN

These little Austrian cookies resemble Danish pastries. The egg yolks are used for firmness.

INGREDIENTS

◊ 2¾ cups all-purpose flour

◊ 1 cup (2 sticks) unsalted butter, softened, cut into pieces

◊ ½ cup superfine sugar

◊ grated zest of 1 lemon

◊ 2 hard-cooked egg yolks

◊ 2 tsp vanilla extract

◊ 1 tbsp rum or brandy

◊ 1 cup blackberry or black plum preserves

◊ 1 egg, separated

◊ sugar for sprinkling

ICING

◊ 1¾ cups confectioners' sugar

◊ 1 to 2 tbsp lemon juice or rum

◊ Into a large bowl, sift flour. Add butter and sprinkle over sugar and lemon zest. Press cooked egg yolks through a strainer over the bowl. Add vanilla extract and brandy, and stir until a dough forms. Knead lightly until dough is well-blended and smooth. Wrap tightly in plastic wrap, and refrigerate 30 minutes.

◊ Preheat oven to 350°F. Lightly grease 2 large baking sheets. On a light floured surface, using a floured rolling pin, roll out half the pastry to ⅛-inch thick rectangle. Using a sharp knife or pastry wheel, cut dough into 3-inch squares. Place 1 teaspoon of preserves in the center of each square, and fold over each corner to the center, overlapping just slightly. Press gently over the preserves. Transfer to the baking sheet.

◊ In a small bowl, beat egg white lightly, and brush over each square; sprinkle each square with a little sugar. Bake until golden brown, 20 to 25 minutes, rotating baking sheets halfway through. Remove baking sheets to wire racks to cool slightly. Then, remove pockets to wire rack to cool completely.

◊ Sift confectioners' sugar into a medium bowl. With a wire whisk, beat in remaining egg white until mixture is smooth. Add a little lemon juice or rum until glaze is a drizzling consistency. Spoon mixture into a paper cone (page 14) and drizzle a little glaze over each cookie.

HANUKKAH SUGAR COOKIES

NOT ILLUSTRATED

ABOUT 3 ½ DOZEN

Search out some unusual cutters for this special
joyous holiday or make your own Jewish star
template from a piece of cardboard!

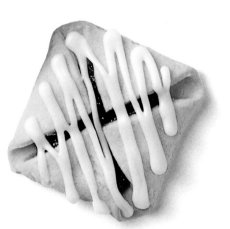

INGREDIENTS

◊ 2¼ cups all-purpose flour
◊ ½ tsp baking powder
◊ ½ tsp salt
◊ ¾ cup (1½ sticks) unsalted butter, softened, or ½ cup unsalted butter and ¼ cup white vegetable shortening
◊ ¾ cup superfine sugar
◊ 1 egg, lightly beaten
◊ grated zest of 1 lemon

◊ 1 tbsp fresh lemon juice
◊ 1 tsp vanilla extract
◊ ½ tsp lemon extract

ICING
◊ 3 cups confectioners' sugar
◊ 2 to 3 tbsp milk
◊ 1 tbsp lemon juice
◊ blue food coloring

◊ Into a medium bowl, sift together flour, baking powder and salt.

◊ In a large bowl with an electric mixer, beat butter or butter and shortening until creamy, 30 to 60 seconds. Add sugar and beat until light and fluffy, 1 to 2 minutes. Gradually beat in egg, lemon zest and juice, and vanilla and lemon extracts until well-blended. On low speed, beat in flour mixture until soft dough forms.

◊ Scrape dough onto a piece of plastic wrap or waxed paper. Using wrap or paper as a guide, shape dough into a flat disk and wrap tightly. Refrigerate several hours or overnight until firm enough to roll (dough can be made up to 2 days ahead).

◊ Preheat oven to 350°F. Lightly grease 2 large baking sheets. On a lightly floured surface, using a floured rolling pin, roll out half the dough ¼ inch thick (keep remaining dough refrigerated). Using floured cutters or template, cut out as many shapes as possible, and arrange 1 inch apart on prepared baking sheets.

◊ Bake until set and golden, 10 to 12 minutes. Remove baking sheets to wire racks to cool slightly. Then, using a metal pancake turner or palette knife, remove cookies to wire racks to cool completely. Repeat with remaining dough and trimmings.

◊ Into a medium bowl, sift confectioners' sugar. Stir in 2 tablespoons milk and lemon juice, adding a little more milk if icing is too thick. Spoon half the icing into a small bowl, and add a few drops of blue food coloring, mixing until you achieve desired shade.

◊ Spoon the icings into 2 separate paper cones (page 14) and pipe designs or decorations onto each cookie shape. Let icing set, about 2 hours. Store in airtight containers with waxed paper between layers.

> **TIP**
> This cookie dough can be rolled out thin, ⅛ inch, for a crisper cookie. The thicker dough in this recipe makes a slightly softer cookie.

CRANBERRY SANDWICH STARS

ABOVE & LEFT

ABOUT 20

These beautiful sandwich cookies are big enough to be a dessert.

INGREDIENTS

- ◊ 2¼ cups all-purpose flour
- ◊ 1½ tsp baking powder
- ◊ ½ tsp ground cinnamon
- ◊ ¼ tsp salt
- ◊ ¾ cup (1½ sticks) unsalted butter, softened
- ◊ ½ cup sugar
- ◊ ¼ cup packed light brown sugar
- ◊ 1 egg, lightly beaten
- ◊ 2 tsp vanilla extract
- ◊ grated zest of 1 lemon

FILLING

- ◊ 1 cup fresh or frozen (defrosted) cranberries
- ◊ 3 tbsp sugar
- ◊ ¾ cup raspberry preserves
- ◊ 1 tbsp lemon juice
- ◊ confectioners' sugar for dusting

◊ Into a medium bowl, sift together flour, baking powder, cinnamon and salt; set aside.

◊ In a large bowl with electric mixer, beat butter until creamy, 30 seconds. Add sugars and beat until light and fluffy, 1 to 2 minutes. Beat in egg, vanilla extract and lemon zest. Stir in flour mixture until a soft dough forms.

◊ Scrape dough onto piece of plastic wrap or waxed paper. Using the wrap or paper as a guide, shape dough into flat disk, and refrigerate until firm enough to roll, 1 to 2 hours.

◊ Lightly grease 2 large non-stick baking sheets. On a lightly floured surface, using a floured rolling pin, roll out one-third of the dough ⅛ inch thick. (Keep remaining dough refrigerated.) Using a 3½-inch star-shaped cutter, cut out an even number of cookies. Using a 1-inch or 1½-inch star-shaped cutter, cut out the center of half the cookies. Arrange cookies on baking sheets ½ inch apart. Refrigerate 15 minutes. Preheat oven to 350°F.

◊ Bake until cookies are just set and edges are golden, 8 to 10 minutes. Remove baking sheets to wire racks to cool slightly. Then remove cookies to wire racks to cool completely.

◊ In a food processor fitted with metal blade, process cranberries, sugar, preserves and lemon juice. Scrape into a medium saucepan, and, over medium heat, cook until mixture is reduced to about 1 cup, 8 to 10 minutes, stirring often. Set aside to cool, stirring occasionally.

◊ Spread about 1 teaspoon cranberry mixture on each whole cookie star to within ½ inch of the edge. Arrange the cut-out cookie stars on a wire rack. Dust liberally with confectioners' sugar; then carefully place over whole stars, gently pressing together. Allow cookies to set 1 hour at room temperature.

> **TIP**
> To dust again with confectioners' sugar before serving, cover the filled centers with small rounds of waxed paper, and dust with confectioners' sugar.

SHREWSBURY BISCUITS

LEFT & ABOVE

ABOUT 3 DOZEN

This traditionally English cookie is flavored with sherry and speckled with dried currants, then dredged with superfine sugar – perfect with tea.

INGREDIENTS

◊ 1 cup (2 sticks) unsalted butter, softened

◊ 1 cup superfine sugar

◊ 1 egg, beaten

◊ ¼ cup heavy cream

◊ 1 tbsp dry sherry

◊ 1 tsp caraway seeds, lightly crushed, (optional)

◊ ½ cup dried currants

◊ 1 to 1¼ cups all-purpose flour, sifted

◊ superfine sugar for sprinkling

◊ In a large bowl with electric mixer, beat butter and sugar until light and creamy, 1 to 2 minutes. Beat in egg, cream, sherry, caraway seeds if using, and currants. Stir in flour until soft dough forms.

◊ Scrape dough onto a piece of plastic wrap or waxed paper and, using wrap or paper as a guide, shape into flat disk and refrigerate until firm, about 1 hour.

◊ Preheat oven to 350°F. Lightly grease 2 large baking sheets. On a lightly floured surface, using a floured rolling pin, roll dough out ¼ inch thick. With a 2½-inch fluted cutter, cut out as many rounds as possible. If you like, reroll trimmings, and cut out more rounds. Place rounds 1 inch apart on prepared baking sheets.

◊ Brush top of cookies with a little water, and sprinkle with a little superfine sugar. Bake until crisp and golden, 15 to 20 minutes. Remove baking sheets to wire racks to cool slightly. Then, using a metal pancake turner, remove cookies to wire racks to cool completely. Store in airtight containers.

ANISE-FLAVOR SUGAR HEARTS

NOT ILLUSTRATED

ABOUT 2 DOZEN

These anise-flavor sugar cookies can be cut into any shape.

INGREDIENTS

◊ 3 cups all-purpose flour

◊ ¾ tsp baking powder

◊ ¼ tsp salt

◊ 1½ tsp aniseed, finely chopped

◊ 1¼ cups (2½ sticks) unsalted butter, softened

◊ 1 cup sugar

◊ 1 egg

◊ 2 tbsp whipping cream

◊ 1 tsp vanilla extract

◊ confectioners' sugar for dusting

◊ Into a medium bowl, sift together flour, baking powder and salt. Stir in chopped aniseed; set aside.

◊ In a large bowl with electric mixer, beat butter until creamy. Add sugar and continue beating until light and fluffy. Beat in egg, cream and vanilla extract until blended. Stir in flour mixture, until blended.

◊ Scrape dough onto piece of plastic wrap and, using wrap as guide, shape into flat disk. Wrap tightly, and refrigerate until firm enough to roll out, 30 minutes.

◊ Preheat oven to 350°F. Lightly butter 2 large baking sheets. On a lightly floured surface, using a floured rolling pin, roll out half the dough about ¼-inch thick. Using a 3½- or 4-inch heart-shaped, floured cookie cutter, cut out as many cookies as possible. Transfer hearts to prepared baking sheet, 1 inch apart.

◊ Bake cookies until they are set and edges are golden, about 8 minutes. Remove baking sheets to wire rack to cool slightly. Then remove cookies to wire racks to cool. Dust cooled cookies with confectioners' sugar.

> **TIP**
> For a delicious dessert, sandwich two heart cookies with anise-scented whipped cream, and top with a few raspberries or blueberries; dust with confectioners' sugar.

CHOCOLATE MACADAMIA WINDMILLS

ABOVE & BELOW

ABOUT 3 DOZEN

These rolled-shaped cookies are rich, yet delicate,
and easy to make.

INGREDIENTS

◊ 2½ cups all-purpose flour

◊ 2 tbsp unsweetened cocoa powder

◊ 2½ tsp baking powder

◊ ½ tsp salt

◊ ½ cup (1 stick) unsalted butter, softened

◊ ½ cup superfine sugar

◊ 1 egg, lightly beaten

◊ 2 tbsp light corn syrup

◊ ½ cup finely chopped macadamia nuts

◊ 3 oz semisweet chocolate, melted

◊ Into a medium bowl, sift together flour, cocoa powder, baking powder and salt.

◊ In a large bowl with electric mixer, beat butter and sugar until light and creamy, 1 to 2 minutes. Beat in egg and syrup until blended; then stir in flour mixture. Turn dough onto lightly floured surface, and knead lightly until smooth. Wrap tightly in plastic wrap or waxed paper, and refrigerate until firm enough to roll, about 30 minutes.

◊ Preheat oven to 350°F. Lightly grease 2 large baking sheets. On a lightly floured surface, using a floured rolling pin, roll out half the dough ⅛-inch thick (keep remaining dough refrigerated). Using a floured 3½-inch round or square cutter, cut as many rounds or squares as possible.

◊ Place cut-outs on baking sheet. Beginning at outside edge, make 4 radial cuts almost to center forming quarters (if a square cutter has been used, cut from each corner). Fold left corner of each quarter to center, and press to seal, forming a windmill shape. Sprinkle center with nuts.

◊ Bake until firm, about 10 minutes. Remove baking sheets to wire racks to cool slightly. Using a metal pancake turner or palette knife, remove cookies to wire racks to cool completely. Repeat with remaining dough and trimmings.

◊ Spoon melted chocolate into paper cone (page 14), and drizzle chocolate in zig-zag pattern over each windmill cookie. Allow chocolate to set. Store cookies in airtight containers with waxed paper between layers.

> **TIP**
> *I*f you don't have 3½-inch round or square cookie cutters, cookies can be cut into 3½-inch squares with a sharp knife or pastry wheel.

CHRISTMAS CUT-OUT COOKIES

LEFT, RIGHT & FAR RIGHT

ABOUT **6** DOZEN
(DEPENDING ON SIZE OF CUTTERS)

These cookies can be cut out in any shapes you can
find: trees, angels, reindeer, bells or stars.

INGREDIENTS

◊ 2 cups all-purpose flour

◊ 2 tsp baking powder

◊ ½ tsp salt

◊ ½ cup (1 stick) unsalted
butter, softened

◊ 1 cup superfine sugar

◊ 1 large egg

◊ grated zest of 1 lemon

◊ 1 tbsp lemon juice

◊ 1 tbsp vanilla extract

◊ ½ tsp lemon extract

ICING

◊ 3 cups confectioners' sugar

◊ 2 to 3 tbsp milk

◊ 1 tbsp lemon juice

◊ red and green food coloring
(optional)

◊ Into a medium bowl, sift together flour, baking
powder and salt. In large bowl with electric mixer, beat
butter until creamy, 30 seconds. Add sugar and
continue beating until light and fluffy, 1 to 2 minutes.
Beat in egg, lemon zest and juice, and vanilla and
lemon extracts until well-blended. Stir in flour
mixture until blended and soft dough forms.

◊ Form dough into a ball, and divide into 3
pieces. Flatten each piece to a disk shape, and
wrap each tightly in plastic wrap. Refrigerate
several hours or overnight until dough is
firm enough to handle.

◊ Preheat oven to 350°F. On a lightly
floured surface, using a floured rolling pin,
roll out one dough disk ⅛-inch thick. Keep
remaining dough disks refrigerated. Using floured
cookie cutters, cut out as many shapes as possible,
and, if necessary using a palette knife, transfer
shapes to 2 large ungreased baking sheets 1 inch
apart.

◊ Bake until cookies are just colored around
the edges, 8 to 10 minutes. Remove baking
sheets to wire racks to cool slightly. Then,
remove cookies to wire racks to cool
completely. Repeat with remaining dough.

◊ Into a medium bowl, sift confectioners' sugar. Stir in
2 tablespoons milk and lemon juice, adding a little more
milk if icing is too thick. Spoon about ⅓ of frosting into
a small bowl and another ⅓ into another small bowl.
Add a few drops of red coloring to one bowl and green
to the other, mixing until you have the desired shades.

◊ Spoon the three colors into three separate paper
cones (page 14). Pipe designs and decorations onto each
cookie. Allow to set about 2 hours, then store in airtight
containers with waxed paper between the layers.

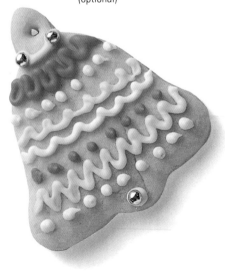

"PRETTY EYES" COOKIES

NOT ILLUSTRATED

ABOUT 2 DOZEN

These Turkish cookies look exotic and taste even better. The dough is rich and short, complemented with any thick preserves.

INGREDIENTS

◊ 1 cup (2 sticks) unsalted butter, softened

◊ 1 cup confectioners' sugar, sifted

◊ 2 tsp vanilla extract

◊ 2½ cups all-purpose flour, sifted

◊ ½ cup apricot or plum preserves

◊ confectioners' sugar for dusting

◊ In a large bowl with electric mixer, beat butter until creamy, 30 to 60 seconds. On low speed, gradually beat in confectioners' sugar, and continue beating until mixture is very light and creamy, 2 minutes. Beat in vanilla extract. Stir in flour and, on a lightly floured surface, knead dough until blended and smooth.

◊ Preheat oven to 350°F. Lightly grease 2 large non-stick baking sheets. On a lightly floured surface, using a floured rolling pin, roll out one half of the dough ¼ inch thick. Using a floured 2-inch star and a crescent-shaped cutter, cut out an even number of each shape. Transfer to baking sheet, and, using a ¼- to ½-inch pastry tip, punch three holes in half the shapes.

◊ Bake cookies until just golden, 10 to 12 minutes. Remove baking sheets to wire racks to cool slightly. Then, using a metal pancake turner or palette knife, remove cookies to wire racks to cool completely. Repeat with remaining dough and trimmings.

◊ In a small bowl, stir preserves to soften; then spread each whole cookie with a little preserve, keeping it toward center. Arrange the hole-punched cookies on a wire rack, and dust generously with confectioners' sugar. Place sugar-dusted tops over preserve-spread bottoms, and press gently so the preserves fill the holes. Allow cookies to set, about 1 hour at room temperature. Store in airtight containers with waxed paper between the layers.

GREEK EASTER COOKIES

NOT ILLUSTRATED

ABOUT 2 ½ DOZEN

These crisp, sugar-topped, cookies are traditionally served in Greece at Easter.

INGREDIENTS

◊ 1⅔ cups all-purpose flour

◊ ¼ tsp salt

◊ ½ tsp ground cinnamon

◊ ½ tsp mixed spice

◊ ⅓ cup dried currants

◊ 2 tbsp chopped candied citron or orange peel

◊ ½ cup (1 stick) unsalted butter, softened

◊ ½ cup sugar

◊ 1 egg, separated

◊ 1 to 2 tbsp milk

◊ sugar for sprinkling

◊ Into medium bowl, sift together flour, salt, cinnamon and mixed spice. Stir in dried currants and candied citron or orange peel, set aside.

◊ In a large bowl with electric mixer, beat butter and sugar until light and creamy, 1 to 2 minutes. Beat in egg yolk until well-blended. Stir in flour mixture, adding milk gradually to form a stiff, smooth dough.

◊ Turn dough onto a lightly floured surface, and knead lightly to blend. Wrap dough in plastic wrap or waxed paper, and refrigerate until dough is firm enough to roll, 15 to 20 minutes.

◊ Preheat oven to 400°F. Lightly grease 2 large baking sheets. On a lightly floured surface, using floured rolling pin, roll out dough to ¼ inch thick. Using a 2½-inch floured, fluted cutter, cut out as many rounds as possible. Reroll trimmings and repeat. Place rounds 1 inch apart on baking sheets.

◊ Bake 8 minutes. Lightly beat egg white, and brush each cookie top. Sprinkle tops with sugar, and return to the oven until cookies are golden and set, about 3 to 5 minutes. Remove baking sheets to wire racks to cool slightly. Then, using a metal pancake turner or palette knife, remove cookies to wire racks to cool completely. Store in airtight containers.

75

CHOCOLATE-ORANGE HEARTS

LEFT & RIGHT

ABOUT 2 ½ DOZEN

These stunning cookies can be made
in any shape – you need three
cutters of the same shape: about a
3¼-, 2⅛- and a 1-inch.

INGREDIENTS

◊ 2 oz semisweet chocolate, chopped

◊ 2¼ cups all-purpose flour

◊ 1½ tsp baking powder

◊ ¼ tsp salt

◊ ¾ cup (1½ sticks) unsalted butter, softened

◊ ¾ cup sugar

◊ 1 egg

◊ 1 tsp vanilla

◊ grated zest of 1 orange

◊ 1 tbsp orange juice

◊ superfine sugar for sprinkling

◊ In a small bowl over a saucepan of simmering water, melt chocolate until smooth. Set aside to cool.

◊ Into a medium bowl, sift together flour, baking powder and salt. In a large bowl with electric mixer, beat butter and sugar until light and creamy, 1 to 2 minutes. Beat in egg, vanilla extract, orange zest and juice until well-blended. On low speed, beat in flour until soft dough forms. Remove half the dough, and wrap tightly in plastic wrap; refrigerate until firm, about 2 hours.

◊ With mixer on low speed, beat melted, cooled chocolate into the dough remaining in bowl. Wrap in plastic wrap, and refrigerate until firm.

◊ Grease and flour 2 or more large baking sheets. On a lightly floured surface, using a floured rolling pin, roll out half the orange-flavor dough ⅛ inch thick (keep remaining dough refrigerated). With a floured, 3¼-inch heart-shaped cutter, cut out as many hearts as possible. Place ½ inch apart on baking sheet and refrigerate. Repeat with chocolate dough, cutting an equal number of chocolate hearts, and place on another baking sheet. Refrigerate until all cut-outs are firm, about 20 minutes.

◊ Preheat oven to 350°F. With a 2⅛-inch floured heart-shaped cutter, carefully cut another heart from center of each 3¼-inch heart. Place smaller orange hearts in larger chocolate hearts and smaller chocolate hearts in larger orange hearts. With a 1-inch heart-shaped cutter, cut small hearts from center of each cookie, and place small orange hearts into medium chocolate hearts, and small chocolate hearts into medium orange hearts.

◊ Sprinkle cookies with a little superfine sugar. Bake cookies until golden, about 10 minutes. Remove baking sheets to wire racks to cool slightly. Then remove cookies to wire racks to cool completely.

TIP
Cookie dough is easier to handle when chilled. If dough becomes too soft to handle, return to refrigerator for a few minutes to firm.

STRAWBERRY PRESERVE SANDWICHES

ABOVE

ABOUT 2 DOZEN

This dough is made with ground almonds for an especially fine-textured cookie.

INGREDIENTS

◊ 1¼ cups blanched almonds

◊ 1½ cups all-purpose flour

◊ ¾ cup (1½ sticks) salted butter, softened

◊ ½ cup superfine sugar

◊ 1 egg, separated

◊ grated zest of 1 lemon

◊ 1 tsp vanilla extract

◊ ½ tsp salt

◊ ½ cup flaked or slivered almonds, chopped

◊ 1 cup strawberry preserves

◊ 1 tbsp lemon juice

◊ In a food processor fitted with metal blade, process blanched almonds and ¼ cup of the flour until very fine. In a large bowl, beat butter until creamy, 30 seconds. Add sugar and continue beating until light and fluffy. Beat in egg yolk, lemon zest and vanilla extract until blended. On low speed, beat in almond mixture, remaining flour and salt until well-blended. Scrape dough onto sheet of waxed paper and, using paper as a guide, form into a flat disk. Refrigerate 2 hours or overnight until dough is firm enough to handle.

◊ Preheat oven to 350°F. Line 2 baking sheets with non-stick baking parchment. On a floured surface, roll half the dough into a rectangle about 12- by 12-inches; keep other half refrigerated. Cut rectangle crosswise into 6 strips, then lengthwise into 6 strips to make 24 2-inch squares. Using a floured ¾-inch round cutter, cut out centers from half the rectangles.

◊ Transfer squares to lined baking sheets ½-inch apart. In a small bowl, whisk egg white until frothy. Brush top of cookie rings only and sprinkle with a few flaked almonds. Bake until just golden, 8 to 10 minutes. Remove baking sheets to wire racks to cool slightly. Remove cookies to wire racks to cool completely.

◊ In a saucepan over low heat, heat strawberry preserves and lemon juice until melted. Spoon a little jam-mixture over the cookie squares; then top with a cookie ring, pressing gently. Allow jam to set firm.

MAPLE LEAF CUT-OUTS

NOT ILLUSTRATED

ABOUT 2 DOZEN

These pretty cookies should be made with natural maple syrup for a rich maple flavor.

INGREDIENTS

◊ 2 cups all-purpose flour

◊ 1 tsp cream of tartar

◊ ½ tsp baking soda

◊ ½ tsp salt

◊ ½ cup butter, softened

◊ ¼ cup packed light brown sugar

◊ ¼ cup natural maple syrup

◊ 1 egg, lightly beaten

◊ Into a medium bowl, sift together flour, cream of tartar, baking soda and salt. In a large bowl with electric mixer, beat butter and sugars until light and fluffy, 1 to 2 minutes. Gradually beat in maple syrup and egg. Add flour and mix until a soft dough forms. Scrape dough into a ball, and flatten slightly. Wrap tightly in plastic wrap, and refrigerate 1 to 2 hours until firm.

◊ Preheat oven to 350°F. Lightly grease 2 large baking sheets. On a lightly floured surface, using a floured rolling pin, roll out half the dough ⅛ inch thick; keep remaining dough refrigerated. Using a floured 3½-inch leaf-shaped cookie cutter, cut out as many shapes as possible. Using the tip of a sharp knife, score surface of leaf shape to resemble veins. Place cookies 1 inch apart on baking sheets.

◊ Bake cookies until lightly colored, 8 to 10 minutes. Remove baking sheets to wire racks to cool slightly. Then, using a metal pancake turner or palette knife, remove cookies to wire racks to cool completely. Repeat with remaining dough rerolling trimmings. Store in airtight containers.

> **TIP**
> *I*f you cannot find a leaf cutter, you can make a simple template from a piece of card and cut around the shape.

DOUBLE CHOCOLATE MINT SANDWICH COOKIES

LEFT & RIGHT

ABOUT 2 DOZEN

A delicious combination of mint-flavored white chocolate ganache sandwiched between thin cocoa-cookie wafers, glazed with dark chocolate.

INGREDIENTS

◇ 1 cup all-purpose flour

◇ ¼ cup unsweetened cocoa powder

◇ ½ cup (1 stick) unsalted butter, softened

◇ ¼ cup sugar

◇ 1 egg

◇ 1 tsp mint extract

WHITE CHOCOLATE FILLING

◇ ½ cup whipping cream

◇ 7 oz fine-quality white chocolate, chopped

◇ 1 tsp mint extract

GLAZE

◇ 5 oz bittersweet or semisweet chocolate, chopped

◇ 3 oz unsalted butter, cut into pieces

◇ Into a medium bowl, sift together flour and cocoa powder. In a large bowl with electric mixer, beat butter and sugar until light and fluffy, 1 to 2 minutes. Beat in egg and mint extract until blended. On low speed, beat in flour-cocoa mixture until soft dough forms.

◇ Scrape dough onto a piece of plastic wrap or waxed paper and, using wrap or paper as a guide, shape dough into a flat disk. Wrap tightly and refrigerate 1 to 2 hours or overnight until firm.

◇ Preheat oven to 350°F. Lightly grease 2 large baking sheets. On a lightly floured surface, using a floured rolling pin, roll out half the dough to ⅛ inch or thinner if possible. Using a 2½-inch floured flower or other cookie cutter, cut out as many cookies as possible. (Be sure to end up with an even number of cookies.)

◇ Bake until edges are set, 6 to 8 minutes; do not overbake as cookies may dry out or burn. Remove baking sheets to wire racks to cool slightly. Then, using a metal pancake turner or palette knife, remove cookies to wire racks to cool completely. Repeat with remaining dough and trimmings.

◇ In a medium saucepan over medium heat, bring whipping cream to a boil. Remove from heat and add white chocolate all at once, stirring constantly until melted and smooth. Stir in mint extract, and strain into a bowl. Cool until firm but not hard, about 1 hour.

◇ With wooden spoon or electric mixer, beat white chocolate filling to lighten, 30 to 45 seconds. Spread a little filling onto half the cookies, and immediately cover with another cookie, pressing together gently, continuing until all cookies are sandwiched. Allow to set 2 hours at room temperature.

◇ In a small saucepan over low heat, melt chocolate and butter for glaze, stirring until smooth. Remove from heat. Cool until thickened to spreading consistency, 20 to 30 minutes. Using a small palette knife, spread a small amount of glaze onto top of each sandwiched cookie, smoothing tops. Refrigerate until set, 20 to 30 minutes. Store in airtight containers, refrigerated, with waxed paper between layers.

Gingerbread

LEFT & RIGHT

ABOUT 2 DOZEN

This rich, spicy dough can be cut into anything you want: boys, girls, santas and reindeer or hearts and flowers.

INGREDIENTS

◊ 3½ cups all-purpose flour

◊ 1 tsp salt

◊ 1 tsp baking powder

◊ 1½ tsp ground ginger

◊ 1½ tsp ground cinnamon

◊ 1½ tsp allspice

◊ 1 tsp ground cloves

◊ ½ tsp finely ground white pepper

◊ 1 cup (2 sticks) unsalted butter or margarine, softened

◊ ⅔ cup packed dark brown sugar

◊ ½ cup light molasses

◊ 1 egg

ROYAL ICING

◊ 2½ cups confectioners' sugar

◊ ¼ tsp cream of tartar

◊ 2 egg whites

◊ food coloring (optional)

◊ 1 tbsp lemon juice or rum

◊ Into a large bowl, sift together flour, salt, baking powder, ginger, cinnamon, allspice, cloves and pepper; set aside.

◊ In a large bowl with electric mixer, beat butter or margarine and brown sugar until light and fluffy, 1 to 2 minutes. Beat in molasses and egg until well-blended. On low speed, beat in flour mixture until soft dough forms.

◊ Scrape dough into a piece of plastic wrap or waxed paper and, using wrap or paper as a guide, shape into a flat disk. Wrap tightly, and refrigerate several hours or overnight until firm enough to roll. (Dough can be made up to 2 days ahead.)

◊ Preheat oven to 350°F. Lightly grease 2 large baking sheets. On a lightly floured surface, using a floured rolling pin, roll out half the dough ¼ inch thick (keep remaining dough refrigerated). With a floured 4-inch gingerbread boy or girl cutter, cut out as many cookies as possible. Arrange cookies 1 inch apart on baking sheet.

◊ Bake until edges are lightly browned 10 to 12 minutes. Remove baking sheets to wire racks to cool slightly. Then, using a metal pancake turner or palette knife, remove cookies to wire racks to cool completely. Repeat with remaining dough and trimmings.

◊ Into a medium bowl, sift together confectioners' sugar and cream of tartar. With an electric mixer, beat in egg whites until well-mixed; then increase speed, and continue beating until stiff and beaters leave a clean path in bottom of bowl. If you like, divide icing into small bowls, and add a few drops of food coloring to each portion of the icing. Add a little lemon juice or rum to achieve a spreading consistency. Spoon icing or icings into one or more paper cones (page 14), and pipe decorations onto gingerbread people. Allow to dry 2 hours at room temperature. Store in airtight containers.

> **TIP**
> To keep icing from drying out while decorating gingerbread, cover bowls tightly with plastic wrap.

VANILLA-CREAM CHEESE CUT-OUTS

NOT ILLUSTRATED

ABOUT 3 DOZEN

According to my friend Marilyn who gave me this recipe, these tender cookies don't need anything other than the little sugar and nut topping.

INGREDIENTS

◊ ½ cup (1 stick) unsalted butter, softened

◊ 1 3-oz package cream cheese, softened

◊ 1 cup less 2 tbsp all-purpose flour

◊ 1 cup confectioners' sugar, sifted

◊ 1 tsp vanilla extract

TOPPING

◊ 1 tbsp superfine sugar

◊ 1 tsp ground cinnamon

◊ 2 tbsp finely chopped almonds

◊ 1 egg

◊ In a large bowl, with electric mixer, beat butter, cream cheese, flour, sugar and vanilla extract until a soft dough forms.

◊ Scrape dough out onto a piece of plastic wrap or waxed paper, and, using wrap or paper as a guide, form into a flat disk shape. Refrigerate until firm.

◊ Line 2 large baking sheets with non-stick baking parchment. On a lightly floured surface, using a floured rolling pin, roll out half the dough ⅛ inch thick. (Keep remaining dough refrigerated.) Using a floured, fluted edge 1½- to 2-inch cutter, cut out as many rounds as possible. (If dough becomes too soft to handle, return to refrigerator until firmer.) Arrange 1 inch apart on prepared baking sheets. Repeat with remaining dough and trimmings. Refrigerate 15 minutes.

◊ Preheat oven to 350°F. In a small bowl, stir together superfine sugar, cinnamon and nuts. In another small bowl, beat egg with 1 tablespoon cold water. Brush tops of cookies with a little of the egg glaze; then sprinkle with a little of the sugar-nut mixture. Bake until just golden, 10 to 12 minutes. Remove baking sheets to wire racks to cool slightly. Then remove cookies to wire racks to cool completely. Store in airtight containers with waxed paper between layers.

SCHNECKENS

RIGHT

ABOUT 4 DOZEN

Years ago my friend Marie gave me this recipe, saying it was an old German cookie her mother used to make. It is simple yet most delicious.

INGREDIENTS

◊ 1 cup unsalted butter, softened

◊ 1 8-oz package cream cheese

◊ 2 cups less 2 tbsp all-purpose flour

◊ ½ tsp salt

◊ ¼ cup sugar

◊ 1 tsp ground cinnamon

◊ ¾ cup raisins

◊ ½ cup chopped walnuts, pecans or hazelnuts

GLAZE

◊ 1 cup confectioners' sugar

◊ 1 tsp lemon juice or water

◊ In a large bowl with electric mixer, beat butter and cream cheese until creamy, 30 to 40 seconds. On low speed, beat in flour and salt until well-blended. Scrape onto a piece of plastic wrap or waxed paper, and, using wrap or paper as a guide, shape into a flat disk. Refrigerate several hours until firm.

◊ On a lightly floured surface, using a lightly floured rolling pin, roll out dough to a rectangle ⅛ inch thick. Sprinkle with sugar and cinnamon, and then raisins and nuts. Starting at a short end, roll dough tightly, jelly-roll fashion, and wrap tightly in plastic wrap. Refrigerate 1 hour.

◊ Preheat oven to 350°F. Lightly grease 2 large baking sheets. Using a sharp knife, cut dough into ½-inch crosswise slices and place 1½ inches apart on baking sheets. Bake until golden and slightly puffed, 12 to 15 minutes. Remove baking sheets to wire racks to cool slightly. Using a metal pancake turner or palette knife, remove cookies to wire racks to cool completely.

◊ Arrange cookies cut-side up close together on wire rack. Into a medium bowl, sift confectioners' sugar. Beat in lemon juice or water to form a glaze, adding a few more drops of water if necessary. With a teaspoon or paper cone (page 14), drizzle glaze over cookies. Allow to set, 30 minutes. Store in airtight containers with waxed paper between layers.

CHAPTER 5

PRESSED AND PIPED Cookies

These cookies are formed by

pressing the dough through a cookie press

or pastry bag and nozzle.

REAL VANILLA BUTTER COOKIES

ABOVE & RIGHT

ABOUT 2 DOZEN

These cookies are a Danish specialty. They use real vanilla seeds from a bean, but you can use a good-quality vanilla extract, although they won't be quite as authentic.

INGREDIENTS

◊ 2 cups less 2 tbsp all-purpose flour

◊ 2 tbsp cornstarch

◊ 5 tbsp sugar

◊ ⅓ cup blanched almonds, finely chopped

◊ ½ vanilla bean or 1 tsp vanilla extract

◊ 1 cup unsalted butter, cut into small pieces

◊ 1 egg, separated

◊ sugar for sprinkling

◊ confectioners' sugar for dusting

◊ Preheat oven to 400°F. Lightly grease 2 large baking sheets. Into a large bowl, sift together flour and cornstarch; stir in sugar and almonds.

◊ Using a sharp knife, split vanilla bean and scrape out seeds. Add to flour mixture and mix well. (If using vanilla extract, mix with egg yolk and add later.)

◊ Using a pastry blender or electric mixer on slow speed, rub butter into flour until fine crumbs form. In a small bowl, beat egg yolk (and vanilla extract, if using). Add to flour-butter mixture and knead until soft but firm dough forms. (If dough is very sticky, sprinkle over a little more flour.)

◊ Spoon dough into a large pastry bag fitted with a large plain tip, and pipe 2-inch "doughnut" shapes 1½ inches apart on baking sheets. In a small bowl, beat egg white until foamy, and brush each ring. Sprinkle with sugar.

◊ Bake until lightly golden and set, 8 to 10 minutes. Remove baking sheets to wire racks to cool slightly. Then, using a metal pancake turner, remove cookies to wire racks to cool completely. Dust with confectioners' sugar. Store in airtight containers.

CAT'S TONGUES

NOT ILLUSTRATED

ABOUT 5 DOZEN

These crisp, not too sweet, cookies are a French classic. They are very elegant served with ice creams, sorbets and fruit salads.

INGREDIENTS

◊ ½ cup (1 stick) unsalted butter, softened

◊ ½ cup superfine sugar

◊ ½ tsp vanilla extract

◊ ¼ tsp salt

◊ 3 egg whites

◊ 1 cup all-purpose flour, *sifted twice*

◊ Preheat oven to 400°F. Lightly grease and flour at least 4 baking sheets. (As you pipe one, begin to bake and recycle baking sheets if necessary – but try to pipe batter all at once.)

◊ In a large bowl with electric mixer, beat butter until creamy, 30 seconds. Add sugar, salt and vanilla extract, and continue beating until light and fluffy, 1 to 2 minutes. Gradually beat in egg whites, beating well after each addition. Gently fold in flour.

◊ Spoon batter into a large pastry bag fitted with a ¼-inch plain tip. In 2 rows, pipe batter in 3-inch long pencil strips, 1½ inches apart, on baking sheets (cookies will spread).

◊ Bake until edges are golden but centers remain pale, 8 to 10 minutes. Remove baking sheets from oven and use a metal pancake turner to remove cookies to wire racks before they crisp up too much on baking sheets, or they may crack; they are fragile.

> ### VARIATION
> Melt about 4 oz bittersweet or semisweet chocolate chopped. Spoon into a paper cone (page 14), and pipe a thin strip, about ⅛- to ¼-inch wide, of melted chocolate down center of a cookie. Sandwich with a second cookie, pressing very gently or chocolate will squeeze out the sides. Allow to set at room temperature, or refrigerate on a baking sheet, 10 to 15 minutes. Store in airtight containers with waxed paper between layers.

CHOCOLATE VIENNESE "S" COOKIES

L E F T & R I G H T

A B O U T 2 D O Z E N

This Viennese cookie is butter-rich and full of chocolate flavor. The classic shape is accentuated by dipping into chocolate.

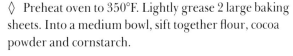

INGREDIENTS

◊ 2 cups all-purpose flour

◊ ⅓ cup unsweetened cocoa powder, preferably Dutch-processed

◊ ¼ cup cornstarch

◊ 1 cup (2 sticks) unsalted butter, softened

◊ ½ cup confectioners' sugar, sifted

◊ 1 tsp vanilla extract

◊ confectioners' sugar for dusting

◊ 4 oz bittersweet or semisweet chocolate, melted

◊ Preheat oven to 350°F. Lightly grease 2 large baking sheets. Into a medium bowl, sift together flour, cocoa powder and cornstarch.

◊ In a large mixing bowl with electric mixer, beat butter and confectioners' sugar until light and fluffy, 1 to 2 minutes. On low speed, gradually beat in flour mixture and vanilla extract until soft dough forms.

◊ Spoon dough into a large pastry bag fitted with a large star tip. Pipe about 24 3-inch "S" shapes or fingers 2 inches apart on prepared baking sheets.

◊ Bake until set and and slightly firm when touched with fingertip, 15 to 20 minutes, rotating baking sheets from top to bottom shelf and from front to back, halfway through cooking time. Remove baking sheets to wire racks to cool until firm, about 15 minutes. Then remove cookies to wire racks to cool completely.

◊ Arrange cookies close together on wire rack and dust with confectioners' sugar. Dip one end of each cookie halfway into melted chocolate. Place on waxed paper-lined baking sheet and allow to set, 30 minutes. Store cookies in airtight containers with waxed paper between layers.

> **TIP**
> Alternatively, dip each cookie into melted chocolate and place on waxed paper-lined baking sheet to set, 30 minutes. Cover chocolate-coated ends of cookies with a strip of waxed paper or foil and carefully dust the center of the cookies with confectioners' sugar.

APRICOT THUMBPRINTS

A B O V E & B E L O W

A B O U T 4 ½ D O Z E N

These classic cookies get their name from the
method of using a thumb to create a round
depression. The hole can be filled with any
preserves you like.

VARIATION

*F*or a fancier
shape, use a
large rosette tip to
pipe cookie dough
and use the handle
of a wooden spoon
to make a more
even-shaped hole
to fill with
preserves.

INGREDIENTS

◊ ¾ cup (1½ sticks) unsalted
butter, softened

◊ ½ cup sugar

◊ 2 eggs, lightly beaten

◊ 1 tsp vanilla extract

◊ ½ tsp ground cinnamon

◊ ¼ tsp salt

◊ 2 cups all-purpose flour

◊ ⅔ cup apricot preserves or
other favorite preserves or jelly

◊ Preheat oven to 400°F. In a large bowl with electric
mixer, beat butter until creamy, 30 seconds. Add sugar
and beat until light and fluffy, 1 to 2 minutes. Gradually
beat in eggs, vanilla extract, cinnamon and salt. Stir in
flour until soft dough forms.

◊ Spoon dough into a large pastry bag fitted with a
plain ½-inch tip. Pipe 1½-inch rounds, 1 inch apart, on
2 large ungreased baking sheets. Press lightly floured
thumb into center of each round, making a deep
depression.

◊ Bake cookies until golden, 7 to 10 minutes. Remove
baking sheets to wire racks to cool slightly. Then, using a
metal pancake turner, remove cookies to wire racks to
cool completely.

◊ In a small saucepan over low heat, heat apricot
preserves until just beginning to bubble. Using a small
teaspoon, spoon a little apricot preserve into each
indentation while cookies are still warm. Allow cookies
and jam to set and cool completely. Store in airtight
containers in single layers.

TIP

*F*or a more
colorful
selection, use 2 or
more different
flavor preserves,
such as apricot,
raspberry and
grape jelly.

CHOCOLATE-DIPPED LEMON RIBBONS

LEFT & RIGHT

ABOUT **3** DOZEN

These lovely-looking and delicious cookies can be made with orange zest and juice replacing the lemon for a tangier flavor.

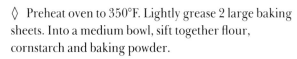

INGREDIENTS

◊ ¾ cup all-purpose flour

◊ 2 tbsp cornstarch

◊ ⅛ tsp baking powder

◊ ½ cup (1 stick) unsalted butter, softened

◊ ⅓ cup confectioners' sugar

◊ 1 egg, separated

◊ grated zest of 1 lemon

◊ 1 tbsp fresh lemon juice

◊ ½ tsp vanilla extract

◊ ⅛ tsp salt

◊ sugar for sprinkling

◊ 3 to 4 oz semisweet chocolate, melted

◊ Preheat oven to 350°F. Lightly grease 2 large baking sheets. Into a medium bowl, sift together flour, cornstarch and baking powder.

◊ In a large bowl with electric mixer, beat butter and sugar until light and fluffy, 1 to 2 minutes. Beat in egg yolk, lemon zest, lemon juice and vanilla extract until well-blended. Stir in flour mixture until well-blended; set aside.

◊ In a small bowl with electric mixer with cleaned beaters, beat egg white and salt until stiff peaks form. Gently fold into butter-flour mixture until soft dough forms.

◊ Spoon dough into a pastry bag fitted with a ribbon tip. Pipe 1½-inch lengths 1 inch apart on prepared baking sheets, and sprinkle each cookie with a little sugar.

◊ Bake until set and edges are golden, 10 to 12 minutes. Remove baking sheets to wire racks to cool, 3 to 5 minutes. Then, using a metal pancake turner, remove to wire racks to cool completely.

◊ Dip each cookie one-third of the way into melted chocolate, and place on waxed paper-lined baking sheet. Allow chocolate to set. Store cookies in airtight containers, with waxed paper between layers.

ORANGE SPRITZ BARS

NOT ILLUSTRATED

ABOUT 8 DOZEN

These spritz bars can be made with any plain spritz cookie dough and filled with your favorite preserve.

INGREDIENTS

◊ 3 cups all-purpose flour

◊ ½ tsp mixed spice

◊ ¼ tsp salt

◊ 1½ cups (3 sticks) unsalted butter

◊ ¾ cup superfine sugar

◊ 1 egg

◊ grated zest of 1 orange

◊ ¼ cup freshly squeezed orange juice

◊ ½ tsp almond extract

◊ 1 cup orange marmalade

◊ flaked almonds to decorate, optional

◊ Into a medium bowl, sift together flour, mixed spice and salt. In a large bowl with electric mixer, beat butter until creamy, 30 to 60 seconds. Add sugar and continue beating until light and fluffy. Beat in egg, orange zest and juice until well-blended. On low speed, beat in flour mixture until well-blended.

◊ Preheat oven to 375°F. Divide dough into quarters. Working with one quarter at a time, fill a cookie press fitted with a ribbon or bar plate. Press 12-inch strips, overlapping lengthwise, onto one side of an ungreased baking sheet, making a base about 3 inches wide. Pat down strips to flatten. Refill press with dough if necessary, and press a border along each side of strips, leaving shallow trough in center. Press out a little dough and use to make 2 ends (this will prevent marmalade from oozing onto baking sheet).

◊ Bake strips 15 minutes. Remove baking sheets from oven. Using back of a spoon, press down center trench of each strip, and fill with marmalade to just below edges.

◊ Return baking sheet to oven, and bake until edges of dough are golden and marmalade is bubbling, 10 to 12 minutes. Remove baking sheets to wire rack to set, about 3 minutes. Using another baking sheet or long metal spatula, slide each long strip onto wire racks to cool, about 5 minutes. Slide each one onto work surface and while still warm, trim edges and cut into 1-inch slices.

SPIRAL SPICE COOKIES

ABOVE & RIGHT

ABOUT 2 DOZEN

These spicy cookies can be piped in easy mounds but the spiral shape looks so pretty.

INGREDIENTS

◊ 1½ cups all-purpose flour

◊ ½ tsp baking soda

◊ 1 tsp ground cinnamon

◊ ½ tsp ground ginger

◊ ½ tsp ground cardamom

◊ ¼ tsp finely ground black pepper

◊ ⅛ tsp salt

◊ ⅓ cup white vegetable shortening

◊ ⅓ cup sugar

◊ ⅓ cup molasses

◊ 1 egg

◊ 2 tbsp cider vinegar

◊ confectioners' sugar for dusting

◊ Into a medium bowl sift together flour, baking soda, cinnamon, ginger, cardamom, pepper and salt.

◊ In a large bowl with electric mixer, beat shortening and sugar until light and fluffy, 1 to 2 minutes. Beat in molasses, egg and vinegar until blended. On low speed, beat in flour-spice mixture until soft dough forms.

◊ Preheat oven to 350°F. Lightly grease 2 large baking sheets. Spoon dough into a large pastry bag fitted with a ¼-inch plain tip. Pipe dough into 2-inch circles, beginning at a center point and working to outer edge, 2 inches apart, on baking sheets.

◊ Bake until just golden, 8 to 10 minutes. Remove baking sheets to wire racks to cool slightly. Then, using a metal pancake turner, remove cookies to wire racks to cool completely. Lightly dust with confectioners' sugar. Store in airtight containers.

MERINGUE CREAM SANDWICHES

LEFT & RIGHT

18 SANDWICHES OR 36 MERINGUES

INGREDIENTS

◊ 4 egg whites

◊ ⅛ tsp cream of tartar

◊ 1¼ cups superfine sugar

◊ 1 tsp vanilla extract

◊ 1 cup heavy or whipping cream

◊ 1 tsp vanilla extract

◊ Preheat oven to 200°F. Line 2 large baking sheets with foil.

◊ In a large bowl with electric mixer, beat egg whites until foamy. Add cream of tartar and continue beating on high speed until soft peaks form. Gradually add sugar a tablespoon at a time, and beat well until whites are stiff and glossy; beat in vanilla extract.

◊ Gently spoon mixture into a large pastry bag fitted with a medium or large star tip. Pipe an even number of 1½- to 2-inch rosettes, 1½ inches apart, on foil-lined baking sheets.

◊ Bake meringues until set and cooked through, about 1 hour, rotating baking sheets from top to bottom shelf and front to back halfway through cooking time. (Do not allow meringues to color.) Turn off oven but leave meringues in oven 1 hour more to continue drying. Remove baking sheets from oven and peel meringues off foil. Arrange meringues on wire racks to cool.

◊ In a medium bowl, whip cream and vanilla extract until peaks form. Spread a little cream on one meringue and sandwich with another.

> **TIP**
>
> Unfilled meringues can be stored in airtight containers.
>
> For a special occasion, omit vanilla extract and add 1 to 2 tablespoons kirsch or a favorite liqueur such as orange or raspberry.

CHOCOLATE SPRITZ SHELLS

NOT ILLUSTRATED

ABOUT 4½ DOZEN

These rich chocolate spritz cookies are piped, but alternatively the dough can be turned through a cookie press.

INGREDIENTS

◊ 2 oz (2 squares) unsweetened chocolate, chopped

◊ ½ cup unsalted butter, softened

◊ 1 cup superfine sugar

◊ ¼ tsp salt

◊ 1 egg

◊ 1 tsp vanilla extract

◊ 2 tbsp milk

◊ 2 cups all-purpose flour, sifted

◊ silver dragées for decorating

◊ Preheat oven to 350°F. In a medium bowl, set over a saucepan of hot water, melt chopped chocolate over low heat until smooth, stirring frequently. Remove from heat, and set aside to cool.

◊ In a large bowl with electric mixer, beat butter until creamy, 30 seconds. Add sugar and salt, and continue beating until light and fluffy, 1 to 2 minutes. Beat in egg, vanilla extract and milk until blended; then slowly beat in cooled chocolate until well-blended. On low speed, beat in flour until soft dough forms. Add a little more flour if dough is too soft (see page 95).

◊ Spoon cookie dough into a large pastry bag fitted with a large star tip, and pipe 2-inch shells on 2 large, cold, ungreased baking sheets, 1½ inches apart. Decorate tips with silver dragées and bake until set and edges are crisp, 8 to 10 minutes. Remove baking sheets to wire racks and, before cookies cool and crisp, use a thin metal palette knife to remove them to wire racks to cool completely. Clean and chill baking sheets, and repeat with remaining cookie dough.

> **TIP**
>
> This cookie dough can be turned through a cookie press with the design plate of your choice; a saw-tooth ribbon plate is especially attractive. Dust with confectioners' sugar.

CHOCOLATE AMARETTI

RIGHT & BELOW

ABOUT 2 DOZEN

These delicious macaroon-like cookies combine the flavors of chocolate and almond. They are surprisingly easy to make. Ideal with an espresso coffee!

◊ 1 cup blanched whole almonds

◊ ½ cup superfine sugar

◊ 1 tbsp unsweetened cocoa powder, preferably Dutch-processed

◊ 2 tbsp confectioners' sugar

◊ 2 egg whites

◊ ⅛ tsp cream of tartar

◊ ½ tsp vanilla extract

◊ ½ tsp almond extract

◊ confectioners' sugar for dusting

◊ Preheat oven to 350°F. Spread almonds on a small baking sheet, and toast until golden and fragrant, 7 to 10 minutes, cool completely. Reduce oven temperature to 325°F. Line a large baking sheet with non-stick baking parchment or lightly greased foil.

◊ In a food processor fitted with metal blade, process almonds with 2 tablespoons of the superfine sugar until finely ground, but not oily. Add cocoa powder and confectioners' sugar, and, using pulse action, process to blend well.

◊ In a medium bowl, beat egg whites, until foamy. Add cream of tartar and continue beating until stiff peaks form. Sprinkle in remaining superfine sugar, a tablespoon at a time, beating well after each addition until whites are stiff and glossy. Beat in vanilla and almond extracts; then gently fold in almond-cocoa mixture until just blended.

◊ Spoon mixture into a large pastry bag fitted with a medium plain ½-inch tip. Pipe 1½-inch mounds 1 inch apart on prepared baking sheets.

◊ Bake until cookies are firm on top when touched with fingertip and surface is slightly crisp, 12 to 15 minutes. Remove baking sheets to wire racks to cool slightly. Then, using a metal pancake turner, remove cookies to wire racks to cool completely. Dust with confectioners' sugar and store in airtight containers.

> **TIP**
> Alternatively, press a sliced blanched almond, round side up, onto center of each mound before baking.

MOCHA MERINGUE STARS

NOT ILLUSTRATED

ABOUT 3 ½ DOZEN

These unusual meringue cookies are made with cocoa and coffee powders for a sophisticated mocha flavor.

INGREDIENTS

◊ 2¼ cups confectioners' sugar, sifted

◊ 1½ tsp unsweetened cocoa powder, preferably Dutch-processed

◊ 1 tsp instant espresso powder (*not* granules)

◊ 4 egg whites

◊ ¼ tsp cream of tartar

◊ 1 tsp vanilla extract

◊ Line 2 large baking sheets with foil. Into a small bowl, sift together ¼ cup of the confectioners' sugar, and the cocoa and espresso powders; set aside.

◊ Preheat oven to 200°F. In a large bowl with electric mixer, beat egg whites on low speed until foamy. Add cream of tartar and continue beating until soft peaks form. Gradually add remaining confectioners' sugar, a tablespoon at a time, beating well after each addition, until whites are stiff and glossy, 10 to 14 minutes. Beat in vanilla extract. Add sugar-cocoa mixture, and fold into whites until just blended.

◊ Spoon meringue mixture into a large pastry bag fitted with medium star tip. Pipe 2½-inch star shapes, 1½ inches apart, onto prepared baking sheets. Bake cookies 1 hour. Turn off oven, but leave meringues in oven 1 hour more to continue drying. Remove baking sheets from oven and peel foil off meringues. Cool completely on wire racks. Store in airtight containers.

> **TIP**
> *F*or even-sized stars, use a star-cutter as a guide; place cutter on foil and gently make a mark at each tip in rows on the foil.

MERINGUE FINGERS

ABOVE & BELOW

ABOUT 3 ½ DOZEN

The grated chocolate cuts the sweetness of these lovely speckled meringues. Dipping in chocolate adds a sophisticated effect.

INGREDIENTS

◊ 2 oz (2 squares) unsweetened chocolate, chopped

◊ ⅓ cup confectioners' sugar, sifted

◊ 4 egg whites

◊ ¼ tsp cream of tartar

◊ 1¼ cups superfine sugar

◊ 1 tsp vanilla extract

◊ cocoa for dusting

◊ Line 2 large baking sheets with foil. In a food processor fitted with metal blade, process chocolate with confectioners' sugar very finely. Pour into a small bowl and refrigerate until ready to add to meringues.

◊ In a large bowl with electric mixer on low speed, beat whites until foamy. Add cream of tartar, and beat on high speed until soft peaks form. Gradually add superfine sugar, a tablespoon at a time, beating well after each addition until whites are stiff and glossy, 10 to 15 minutes. Gently fold in chocolate mixture until just blended.

◊ Preheat oven to 200°F. Spoon mixture into a large pastry bag fitted with a medium star tip. Pipe 3-inch fingers or "S" shapes 1½ inches apart on prepared baking sheets.

◊ Bake meringues 1 hour. Turn off oven but do not remove meringues. Leave meringues in oven 1 hour more. Remove baking sheets from oven and peel off foil. Arrange meringues on wire racks to cool completely. Dust with cocoa if you like.

◊ In a small bowl set over a saucepan of simmering water, melt chocolate until smooth, stirring frequently. Remove from heat. Dip one end of each cookie into melted chocolate and place on waxed paper-lined baking sheet. Allow to set until firm, about 1 hour. Store in airtight containers with waxed paper between layers.

MERINGUE MUSHROOMS

ABOVE & BELOW

ABOUT 3 DOZEN

These little cookies never fail to please. In France they are used to decorate the Christmas log, *Buche de Noël*.

INGREDIENTS

◊ 3 egg whites

◊ ⅛ tsp cream of tartar

◊ 1¼ cups confectioners' sugar

◊ 2 oz semisweet chocolate, melted

◊ unsweetened cocoa powder for dusting

◊ Line a large baking sheet with foil. In a large bowl with electric mixer on low speed, beat egg whites until foamy. Add cream of tartar, increase speed, and beat until soft peaks form. Gradually add sugar, a tablespoon at a time and beat well until stiff and glossy.

◊ Spoon into a large pastry bag fitted with a ½-inch plain tip. Pipe about 30 1½-inch rounds, resembling mushroom caps, 1½ inches apart on prepared baking sheets. Pipe remaining mixture between rounds into an equal number of ¾- to 1-inch high cone shapes. Allow to sit 1 hour to dry slightly.

◊ Preheat oven to 200°F. Bake meringues 1 hour, rotating baking sheet from front to back halfway through cooking time. Turn off oven, but leave meringues in oven 1 hour more to continue drying. Remove baking sheet to wire rack and peel foil off mushroom caps and stems. With tip of small sharp knife, make a small hole in underside of each cap.

◊ With a small palette knife or round-bladed kitchen knife, spread a little melted chocolate on the underside of a "mushroom cap," and gently push the pointed end of a cone shape into the hole to form the stem. Allow to set at least 1 hour. Dust tops with cocoa powder.

> **TIP**
> Do not be tempted to add sugar to whites too quickly as this may cause meringues to weep and stick.

ANISE PUFFS

NOT ILLUSTRATED

ABOUT 4 DOZEN

Recipes for anise-flavor cookies are found in Italian, German, Austrian and Jewish cookbooks. Anise oil is very strong, so use only a few drops. Caraway seeds are sometimes substituted for anise.

INGREDIENTS

◊ 4 eggs

◊ 1¼ cups sugar

◊ 3 to 4 drops anise oil or lemon extract

◊ 1 tbsp anise seeds, lightly crushed

◊ grated zest of small lemon (optional)

◊ 2½ to 3 cups flour, sifted

◊ Grease 2 large baking sheets *very well*. In a large mixing bowl with electric mixer, beat eggs and sugar until very thick and almost white, and mixture leaves a very thick slow ribbon trail when beaters are lifted from bowl, 30 minutes. Beat in anise oil or lemon extract and anise seeds. On low speed, beat in flour until soft dough forms.

◊ Spoon mixture into a large pastry bag fitted with ¼-inch plain tip. Pipe 1- to 1½-inch mounds onto greased baking sheets. Allow to dry overnight at room temperature.

◊ Preheat oven to 300°F. Bake until puffed and lightly golden, 15 to 20 minutes, rotating baking sheets from top to bottom shelf and from front to back halfway through cooking time. Remove baking sheets to wire racks to cool slightly. Then, using a metal palette knife, remove cookies to baking sheets to cool completely. Store in airtight containers.

> **TIP**
> Do not be tempted to underbeat. These cookies must be beaten for 30 minutes and then dried overnight in order to puff like meringues.

SPRITZ COOKIES

L E F T   &   R I G H T

ABOUT 4 ½ DOZEN

These tender, rich butter cookies are the classic cookie press cookie. They are a Scandinavian-American specialty.

INGREDIENTS

◊ 1 cup (2 sticks) unsalted butter, softened

◊ ½ cup superfine sugar

◊ 1 egg

◊ 1½ tsp vanilla or 1 tsp almond extract

◊ 2¼–2½ cups all-purpose flour, sifted

◊ candied cherries to decorate

◊ Preheat oven to 375°F. In a large bowl with electric mixer, beat butter until creamy, 30 to 60 seconds. Add sugar and continue beating until mixture is light and fluffy, 1 to 2 minutes. Beat in egg and vanilla or almond extract. On low speed, gradually beat in 2¼ cups flour until soft dough forms.

◊ Pack cookie dough into a cookie press fitted with the design plate of your choice. Press out cookies onto 2 *cold* ungreased baking sheets. Press a candied cherry into center of each cookie.

◊ Bake until set and just golden, 7 to 10 minutes. Remove baking sheets to wire racks and before cookies cool and crisp, use a thin metal palette knife to remove them to wire racks to cool completely. Clean and chill baking sheets, and repeat with remaining cookie dough. Store in airtight containers.

TIP

Cookie press cookies can be difficult to form unless the dough is the right temperature. If the dough or weather is too warm, the dough won't hold its shape and may have to be chilled about 30 minutes before pressing. If the dough is chilled too long or is too firm, it will be difficult to press through the design plate. To stiffen dough, add a little more flour. If too stiff, add a little milk. Form a log shape slightly smaller than the diameter of the cookie press and insert into the prepared press. Every cookie press has its own directions, which you should read carefully. You may want to practice with a few turns.

6

BAR Cookies

These cookies are formed by

spreading the dough in a shallow pan and

cutting into bars or squares once it has been baked.

CHOCOLATE-ORANGE DREAM BARS

LEFT & RIGHT

18 OR MORE

This bar cookie is made with one of my favorite combinations, chocolate and orange. They are really rich; a little goes a long way.

INGREDIENTS

CHOCOLATE SHORTBREAD CRUST

◊ 1 cup all-purpose flour

◊ ¼ cup unsweetened cocoa powder, preferably Dutch-processed

◊ ¼ tsp salt

◊ 10 tbsp (1¼ sticks) unsalted butter, softened

◊ ⅓ cup superfine sugar

◊ ⅓ cup confectioners' sugar

ORANGE TOPPING

◊ grated zest of 1 orange

◊ ½ cup fresh orange juice

◊ ¼ cup water

◊ 4 tsp cornstarch

◊ 1 tsp lemon juice

◊ 1 tbsp butter

◊ ½ cup orange marmalade

CHOCOLATE GLAZE

◊ 3 tbsp heavy cream

◊ ½ tsp corn syrup

◊ 3 oz bittersweet or semi-sweet chocolate, chopped

◊ Preheat oven to 325°F. Prepare an 8-inch square baking pan. (See page 102.)

◊ Into a medium bowl, sift together flour, cocoa powder and salt. In a large bowl with electric mixer, beat the butter and sugars until light and creamy, 30 to 60 seconds. On low speed, in 2 or 3 batches, beat in flour mixture until soft dough forms.

◊ If necessary, turn dough out onto a lightly floured surface, and knead lightly to be sure it is well-blended. Pat dough onto bottom of prepared pan in an even layer, smoothing surface. Prick dough bottom all over with a fork.

◊ Bake crust until set and golden, 30 to 35 minutes. Remove to wire rack while preparing topping.

◊ In a medium saucepan, whisk together orange zest, juice, water, cornstarch and lemon juice. Over medium heat, bring to a boil, whisking constantly until mixture thickens, about 1 minute. Remove from heat, and whisk in butter and marmalade until melted and smooth. Pour over warm crust and return to oven. Bake 5 minutes more. Remove to wire rack to cool completely; then refrigerate to set topping, about 1 hour.

◊ In a small saucepan, bring cream and corn syrup to a boil. Remove from heat, and all at once stir in chocolate until melted and smooth. Cool chocolate slightly until thickened, stirring occasionally.

◊ Using foil as a guide, remove from pan. Peel off foil, and on a board cut into bars or squares. Spoon cooled thickened chocolate into a paper cone (page 14), and drizzle bars or squares with chocolate. Refrigerate until chocolate sets, 30 minutes. Store refrigerated in airtight containers in single layers.

TIP

*I*f you like, drizzle chocolate over pan of uncut bars and refrigerate until set. Store covered in the pan and cut into bars as liked.

Golden Apricot Squares

NOT ILLUSTRATED

ABOUT 16

These apricot squares are easy to make and so delicious. Served with a custard sauce, they make a delicious dessert.

INGREDIENTS

ALMOND CRUST

◊ ½ cup (1 stick) unsalted butter, softened

◊ ¾ cup all-purpose flour

◊ ⅓ cup whole blanched almonds, finely ground

◊ ¼ cup sugar

APRICOT TOPPING

◊ 1 cup dried apricots

◊ 1 cup water

◊ 1 cup packed light brown sugar

◊ 2 eggs

◊ ½ cup chopped whole blanched almonds

◊ ⅓ cup all-purpose flour

◊ ½ tsp almond extract

◊ ½ tsp baking powder

◊ ¼ tsp salt

◊ confectioners' sugar for dusting

◊ Preheat oven to 350°F. Grease an 8-inch square baking pan. Into a large bowl with electric mixer at medium speed, beat butter, flour, ground almonds and sugar until well mixed and a crumbly dough forms. With back of a spoon or fingertips, press dough evenly into bottom of pan. Bake until top is slightly puffed and golden, about 25 minutes. Remove pan to wire rack.

◊ In a medium saucepan over high heat, bring apricots and water to a boil. Reduce heat and simmer covered until very soft, 15 to 20 minutes, adding a little more water if necessary. Cool slightly, then drain well and chop finely. Turn into a medium bowl.

◊ To the apricots, add brown sugar, eggs, almonds, flour, almond extract, baking powder and salt. Using electric mixer, beat until light and fluffy, 1 to 2 minutes. Pour over baked crust.

◊ Bake until puffed and golden, about 25 minutes. Remove pan to wire rack to cool completely. Cut into 16 squares, and dust lightly with confectioners' sugar. Store in airtight containers in single layers.

Chocolate Raspberry Macaroon Bars

ABOVE & RIGHT

ABOUT 2 DOZEN

INGREDIENTS

CHOCOLATE SHORTBREAD

◊ ½ cup (1 stick) unsalted butter, softened

◊ ½ cup confectioners' sugar, sifted

◊ ¼ cup unsweetened cocoa powder, preferably Dutch-processed, sifted

◊ ¼ tsp salt

◊ 1 tsp vanilla or almond extract

◊ 1 cup all-purpose flour

TOPPING

◊ ½ cup seedless raspberry preserve

◊ 1 tbsp raspberry-flavor liqueur

◊ 1 cup mini, semisweet chocolate chips

◊ 1½ cups finely ground blanched almonds

◊ 4 egg whites

◊ ¼ tsp salt

◊ 1 cup superfine sugar

◊ ½ tsp almond extract

◊ ¼ cup flaked almonds

◊ Preheat oven to 325°F. Prepare 13- by 9-inch baking pan (see page 102). In a medium bowl with electric mixer, beat butter, confectioners' sugar, cocoa powder and salt until creamy. Beat in vanilla or almond extract, and beat in flour until crumbly dough forms. Turn dough into prepared pan and prick with a fork. Bake until set, about 20 minutes. Remove to wire rack and increase oven to 375°F.

◊ Combine raspberry preserve and liqueur. Spread evenly over macaroon crust; then sprinkle with chocolate chips. In a food processor fitted with metal blade, process ground almonds, egg whites, salt, superfine sugar and almond extract until well-blended and foamy. Gently pour over jam and chocolate chip layer. Sprinkle with flaked almonds.

◊ Bake until top is lightly colored and puffed, 20 to 25 minutes. Remove and cool until firm, about 30 minutes. Remove macaroons, and cool completely on wire rack. Peel off foil and cut into bars.

DATE AND OAT CRUMB SQUARES

LEFT & BELOW

ABOUT 2 DOZEN

If you like dates, this is for you. A delicious, rich, date mixture sandwiched between layers of crumbly oat crust and topping.

INGREDIENTS

FILLING

◊ 1 pound pitted dates

◊ 1 cup packed light brown sugar

◊ ⅔ cup water

◊ 1 tsp vanilla extract

CRUST

◊ 1½ cups old-fashioned oats

◊ 1½ cups all-purpose flour

◊ 1 cup packed light brown sugar

◊ 1 tsp ground cinnamon

◊ ½ tsp baking soda

◊ ½ cup chopped walnuts

◊ 1 cup (2 sticks) cold unsalted butter, cut into small pieces

◊ Prepare 13- by 9-inch baking pan (see page 102).

◊ In a medium saucepan, simmer dates, sugar and water over medium heat until sugar dissolves. Remove from heat, and stir in vanilla extract. Pour into a food processor fitted with metal blade, and process mixture until just smooth. Pour into bowl to cool completely.

◊ Preheat oven to 350°F. In a large bowl, combine oats, flour, brown sugar, cinnamon, baking soda and walnuts. Sprinkle over cut-up butter and, using fingertips, rub in butter until coarse crumbs form.

◊ Turn half of mixture into foil-lined pan, and pat firmly into bottom and sides to form a lower crust, smoothing surface. Spread cooled filling over crust; then sprinkle over remaining crumb mixture, covering filling evenly.

◊ Bake until topping is well browned and filling is sizzling, about 35 minutes. Remove pan to wire rack to cool, about 1 hour. Using foil as a guide, remove cookie mixture from pan, and set on board. Peel off foil, and cut into squares and bars. Store in airtight containers.

> **VARIATION**
> *F*or a fig filling, substitute 1 pound dried figs for dates. Remove stems and prepare as above.

CHOCOLATE HEAVEN

NOT ILLUSTRATED

ABOUT 3 DOZEN

This is a chocolate lover's dream; dark, milk and white chocolate packed with nuts and coconut and raisins on an easy graham cracker-crust base!

INGREDIENTS

GRAHAM CRACKER CRUST

◊ 32 graham crackers

◊ 1 tsp ground cinnamon

◊ ½ tsp ground nutmeg

◊ ¾ cup (1½ sticks) unsalted butter, melted

TOPPING

◊ 1 cup sweetened shredded coconut

◊ ½ cup golden raisins

◊ 2 cups pecan halves, coarsely chopped

◊ 6 oz bittersweet or semisweet chocolate, chopped

◊ 6 oz fine-quality milk chocolate, chopped

◊ 6 oz fine-quality white chocolate, chopped

◊ 1 × 14 oz can sweetened condensed milk

◊ Preheat oven to 350°F. Lightly grease a 15½- by 10½-inch jelly roll pan. In a food processor fitted with metal blade, process graham crackers, cinnamon and nutmeg until even, fine crumbs. (You may need to work in batches.) Pour into a bowl and add the melted butter, tossing to mix well.

◊ With the back of a spoon or fingers, press crumbs evenly onto bottom and ¾-inch up sides of pan. Sprinkle coconut evenly over crust; then sprinkle over golden raisins.

◊ In a large bowl, toss together chopped pecans and 3 kinds of chopped chocolate. Pour over condensed milk, and toss well; then pour over coconut and raisins. Smooth top, distributing nuts and chocolate as evenly as possible.

◊ Bake until chocolate looks soft and liquid is golden and bubbling, 30 to 35 minutes. Remove to wire rack to cool completely. Run a knife around edges to loosen and using 2 metal pancake turners, slide onto a board. Using a sharp knife, cut into 2- by 1½-inch bars. Store in airtight containers in single layers or with waxed paper between layers.

CHOCOLATE HAZELNUT BARS

ABOVE

ABOUT 16

The combination of a shortbread hazelnuts and rich chocolate is almost unbeatable.

INGREDIENTS

HAZELNUT CRUST

◊ ½ cup hazelnuts

◊ ¾ cup all-purpose flour

◊ ⅓ cup sugar

◊ 6 tbsp (¾ stick) cold, unsalted butter, cut into small pieces

CHOCOLATE TOPPING

◊ ½ cup sugar

◊ ¼ tsp salt

◊ ⅓ cup unsweetened cocoa powder, preferably Dutch-processed, sifted

◊ ⅓ cup water

◊ 2 tbsp unsalted butter

◊ 2 eggs

◊ 1½ tsp vanilla extract

◊ confectioners' sugar for dusting

◊ Preheat the oven to 350°F. Place hazelnuts on a baking sheet, and cook until golden and fragrant, 5 to 7 minutes. Pour onto a plate to cool. Prepare an 8-inch square baking pan. (See page 102.)

◊ In a food processor fitted with metal blade, process toasted hazelnuts with flour and sugar until fine crumbs form. Add cut-up butter and, using pulse action, process the mixture until fine crumbs form. Turn mixture into prepared pan, and pat onto bottom of pan, smoothing top evenly. Bake until top is set and lightly colored, 20 to 25 minutes. Remove pan to wire rack.

◊ In a medium saucepan, stir together sugar, salt and cocoa powder. Gradually whisk in water until smooth. Over medium heat, bring to a simmer, stirring until sugar dissolves. Remove from heat, and stir in butter until melted. Allow to cool, about 5 minutes. Beat in eggs and vanilla extract, and pour over baked crust.

◊ Bake until topping is set, about 20 minutes. Remove to wire rack to cool completely. Using foil as a guide, remove from pan and set on board. Cut into 1-inch bars, and dust with confectioners' sugar. Store refrigerated in airtight containers with waxed paper between layers.

BEST CHOCOLATE BROWNIES

A B O V E & B E L O W

ABOUT 2 DOZEN

This is the classic chocolate brownie, dense and fudgy with lots of walnuts. A soft chocolate glaze turns the brownies into an elegant treat.

◊ Preheat oven to 350°F. Prepare a 13- by 9-inch baking pan. In a medium saucepan over low heat, melt chocolate and butter or margarine until completely smooth, stirring frequently. Remove from heat, and stir in sugar until blended. Beat in eggs, one at a time, beating well after each addition. Beat in vanilla extract, nuts and chocolate chips. Stir in flour until just blended; batter will be stiff. Spread in prepared pan.

◊ Bake brownies until a cake tester or toothpick inserted in center comes out with sticky crumbs attached, 30 to 35 minutes. *Do not overbake*. Remove pan to wire rack to cool completely.

◊ In a medium saucepan over low heat, melt chocolate and cream until smooth, stirring frequently. Remove from heat to cool slightly. Whisk in butter and vanilla extract. Dip 24 walnut or pecan halves halfway into chocolate, and place on waxed paper-lined baking sheet to set. Cool remaining glaze until slightly thickened and spreadable.

◊ Using foil as a guide, remove brownies from pan, and invert onto a board or baking sheet. Using a metal palette knife, spread brownies with glaze. Refrigerate until set, at least 1 hour.

◊ Using a long-bladed, sharp knife, cut into 24 squares. Press a walnut or pecan half into center of each brownie square. Store in airtight containers in single layers.

INGREDIENTS

◊ 4 oz unsweetened chocolate, chopped

◊ ¾ cup (1½ sticks) butter or margarine, cut into pieces

◊ 1¾ cups sugar

◊ 3 eggs

◊ 1 tsp vanilla extract

◊ 1½ cups chopped walnuts or pecans

◊ 1 cup semisweet chocolate chips (optional)

◊ 1 cup all-purpose flour

CHOCOLATE GLAZE

◊ 6 oz bittersweet or semisweet chocolate, chopped

◊ ½ cup heavy cream

◊ 2 tbsp unsalted butter, cut into pieces

◊ 1 tsp vanilla extract

◊ 24 walnut or pecan halves to decorate

VARIATION

*I*f you prefer brownies unglazed, refrigerate for 1 hour before cutting into squares. Dust squares with confectioners' sugar or cocoa powder or leave just as they are!

TIP: PREPARING A BAKING PAN

*M*old a sheet of foil over bottom of pan, smoothing evenly around corners. Remove foil and turn pan right side up. Press foil into pan, smoothing into sides and corners. Lightly oil foil.

BLONDIES WITH MILK CHOCOLATE MACADAMIA TOPPING

ABOUT 16

These blondies have a butterscotch flavor with an easy-to-make, chocolate-nut topping. Macadamias are expensive, but they go well with the milk chocolate. If you prefer, use hazelnuts or pecans.

INGREDIENTS

◊ ½ cup (1 stick) unsalted butter, melted

◊ 1½ cups packed light brown sugar

◊ 2 eggs

◊ 1 tsp vanilla extract

◊ 1½ cups all-purpose flour

◊ 2 tsp baking powder

◊ ½ tsp salt

◊ 1 cup semisweet chocolate or butterscotch flavor chips (optional)

◊ 6 oz milk chocolate chips or good-quality milk chocolate, chopped

◊ 1 cup chopped macadamia nuts

◊ Preheat oven 350°F. Lightly grease and flour a 9-inch springform pan.

◊ In a large bowl with electric mixer, beat together butter, sugar, eggs and vanilla extract until well-blended. On low speed, beat in flour, baking powder and salt until well-blended. Stir in chocolate chips, if using.

◊ Turn into prepared pan, and smooth top evenly. Bake until dry on top and cake tester or toothpick inserted in center comes out with a few sticky crumbs attached, about 30 minutes. Remove pan to wire rack. Sprinkle chopped chocolate evenly over top, trying not to touch side of pan. Return to oven to soften chocolate, 1 minute. Use the back of a spoon to spread chocolate evenly. Sprinkle nuts evenly over chocolate and, using a clean spoon, press lightly into chocolate. Cool completely; then refrigerate until chocolate is set.

◊ Using a thin-bladed knife, run knife around side of pan, unclip side and remove. Cut blondie into wedges. Store in airtight containers in single layers.

MAPLE MACADAMIA CHEWIES

ABOUT 2 ½ DOZEN

INGREDIENTS

MAPLE CRUST

◊ ½ cup (1 stick) unsalted butter, softened

◊ ½ cup sugar

◊ 1 egg

◊ 1 tsp natural maple flavor

◊ 1½ cups all-purpose flour

NUT TOPPING

◊ 1 cup packed dark brown sugar

◊ ¼ cup (½ stick) unsalted butter

◊ ¼ cup whipping cream

◊ 3 tbsp corn syrup

◊ 3 tbsp natural maple syrup

◊ 2 cups unsalted macadamia nuts

◊ Prepare a 13- by 9-inch baking pan. (See page 102.) In a medium bowl, beat butter and sugar until light and fluffy, 1 to 2 minutes. Beat in egg and maple flavor. On low speed, beat in flour until just blended. Roll out dough between 2 sheets of waxed paper to a 14- by 10-inch rectangle. Slide onto a baking sheet, and refrigerate 10 minutes.

◊ Preheat oven to 350°F. Remove top sheet of waxed paper, and invert dough into prepared pan. Peel off bottom piece of waxed paper. Press pastry onto bottom of pan and ½ inch up sides. Prick dough with fork. Line pastry with waxed paper or foil, and fill with dried beans or rice. Bake crust for 15 minutes. Remove beans or rice and waxed paper, and bake until top is set and golden, 5 to 7 minutes. Remove pan to wire rack.

◊ In a heavy-bottomed saucepan, whisk together sugar, butter, cream, corn syrup and maple syrup. Over medium heat, bring mixture to a boil, stirring constantly until sugar dissolves; then boil without stirring, 1 minute. Remove from heat, and stir in nuts until well-coated. Pour mixture over crust.

◊ Bake until filling is bubbling and thickened, 10 minutes. Remove to wire rack to cool completely. Using foil as a guide, remove cookie mixture to a board. Peel off foil, and cut into 2- by 1½-inch bars.

ROCKY ROAD SQUARES

ABOVE & BELOW

ABOUT 1 DOZEN

This fantastic combination of chocolate, nuts and marshmallows is a winner. For a delicious dessert, top with store-bought Rocky Road ice cream.

◊ Preheat oven to 350°F. Prepare a 13- by 9-inch baking pan (see page 102).

◊ Into a medium bowl, sift together flour, cocoa powder, baking soda and salt. In a large bowl with electric mixer, beat butter and brown sugar until light and fluffy, 1 to 2 minutes. Beat in eggs and vanilla extract. On low speed, beat in flour-cocoa mixture until blended, then stir in coconut, 2 cups of the chocolate chips and chopped almonds.

◊ Turn dough into prepared pan, and pat or spread mixture evenly onto bottom of pan. Bake until set, but still moist in center, 15 to 17 minutes. Remove pan from oven, and sprinkle top evenly with remaining chocolate chips and mini marshmallows. Return pan to oven, and bake until chocolate chips and marshmallows begin to soften and blend into each other, about 4 minutes. Remove pan to wire rack to cool for 10 minutes.

◊ Using foil as a guide, remove cookie mixture from pan and set on board. Peel off foil and, while still warm, cut into bars or squares. Cool completely on wire rack. Dust lightly with confectioners' sugar. Store in airtight containers with waxed paper between layers.

INGREDIENTS

◊ 1¾ cups all-purpose flour

◊ ¼ cup unsweetened cocoa powder, preferably Dutch-processed

◊ 1 tsp baking soda

◊ ½ tsp salt

◊ 1 cup (2 sticks) unsalted butter, softened

◊ 1 cup packed light brown sugar

◊ 2 eggs, lightly beaten

◊ 1 tsp vanilla extract

◊ ¾ cup sweetened flaked coconut

◊ 3 cups semisweet chocolate chips

◊ 1 cup whole blanched almonds, coarsely chopped

◊ 1 cup mini marshmallows

◊ confectioners' sugar for dusting

SCOTTISH SHORTBREAD

ABOVE & BELOW

16 LARGE WEDGES OR
32 THIN WEDGES

This is the most basic cookie – butter, sugar and
flour – and yet one of the most delicious.
Perfect with a cup of tea.

INGREDIENTS

◊ ¼ cup confectioners' sugar

◊ ¼ cup superfine sugar

◊ ¼ tsp salt

◊ 10 tbsp (1¼ sticks) unsalted
butter, softened

◊ 2½ cups all-purpose flour

◊ Preheat the oven to 275°F. Into a large bowl, sift confectioners' sugar. Add superfine sugar and salt, and mix well. Add butter and, using electric mixer, beat butter and sugars until light and fluffy, 1 to 2 minutes. Stir in flour until blended. On a lightly floured surface, knead dough very lightly to ensure even blending.

◊ Divide dough evenly between two 8-inch cake pans with removable bottoms, and pat onto bottoms in even layers. Using a kitchen fork, press ¾-inch radiating lines around the edge of the dough. Prick the surface lightly with the fork (this helps keep an even surface as well as creating the traditional pattern).

◊ Bake until pale golden (do not brown; shortbread should be very pale), about 1 hour, rotating pans halfway through cooking. Remove pans to wire rack to cool, 10 minutes.

◊ Carefully remove side of each pan, and place pan bottom onto heat-proof surface. Cut each shortbread circle into 8 wide or 16 thin wedges. This must be done while shortbread is warm and soft, or it will break. Return shortbread wedges on their bases to wire racks to cool completely. Store in airtight containers.

> **TIP**
> Scottish Shortbread is sometimes made with part rice flour (about ¼ of the total volume of flour). Rice flour is available at some specialty and health food stores, and can be substituted for part of the flour in the above proportions for an even shorter texture.

HERMITS

NOT ILLUSTRATED

ABOUT 2 DOZEN

In New England the recipes usually contained sour cream; in this Southern version the moisture is provided by the molasses. Use any kind of dried fruits and nuts you like.

INGREDIENTS

◊ 1 cup all-purpose flour

◊ 1½ tsp baking soda

◊ ½ tsp cream of tartar

◊ 1 tsp ground cinnamon

◊ ½ tsp grated or ground nutmeg

◊ ½ tsp ground cloves

◊ ¼ tsp ground mace

◊ ¼ tsp ground allspice

◊ ¾ cup raisins

◊ ¾ cup chopped, pitted dates

◊ ¾ cup chopped, dried apricots

◊ ½ cup (1 stick) butter or margarine, softened

◊ ½ cup sugar

◊ 2 eggs, lightly beaten

◊ ½ cup unsulfured molasses

◊ 1 cup chopped walnuts, pecans or hazelnuts

◊ confectioners' sugar for dusting

◊ Preheat oven to 350°F. Prepare a 13- by 9-inch baking pan. (See page 102.)

◊ Into a medium bowl, sift together flour, baking soda, cream of tartar, cinnamon, nutmeg, cloves, mace and allspice. Place raisins, dates and apricots in a small bowl, and toss with a quarter of flour-spice mixture.

◊ In a large bowl with electric mixer, beat butter and sugar until light and fluffy, 1 to 2 minutes. Gradually beat in eggs and molasses until well-blended. On low speed, beat in flour-spice mixture until blended; then stir in flour-coated fruit and nuts.

◊ Spread batter in foil-lined pan. Bake until top is set, 17 to 20 minutes. Remove pan to wire rack to cool completely. Remove cookie mixture to a board, and peel off foil. Cut into bars and dust with confectioners' sugar. Store in airtight containers with waxed paper between layers.

LEMON BARS

ABOVE & BELOW

ABOUT 30

These bar cookies are simple to make and are absolutely delicious. The combination of buttery shortbread and tart lemon topping is perfect.

INGREDIENTS

SHORTBREAD CRUST

◊ 1½ cups all-purpose flour

◊ ½ cup confectioners' sugar

◊ ½ tsp salt

◊ ¾ cup (1½ sticks) cold unsalted butter, cut into small pieces

◊ 1 tsp grated lemon zest (optional)

LEMON TOPPING

◊ 4 eggs

◊ 1½ cups superfine sugar

◊ grated zest of 1 lemon

◊ ½ cup fresh lemon juice

◊ ¾ cup heavy cream

◊ confectioners' sugar for dusting

◊ Preheat oven to 325°F. Prepare a 13- by 9-inch baking pan (see page 102).

◊ Into a large bowl, sift together flour, sugar and salt. Sprinkle over cut-up butter with lemon zest, if using, and, using a pastry blender or fingertips, cut in butter until coarse crumbs form and mixture sticks together.

◊ Turn crumbs into prepared pan, and press firmly into bottom of pan to form a level base, smoothing top evenly. Bake until just golden, about 20 minutes. Remove pan to wire rack to cool slightly.

◊ In a medium bowl, beat eggs and sugar until fluffy, 3 to 5 minutes. Beat in lemon zest and juice until blended.

◊ In another bowl with cleaned beaters, beat cream until soft peaks form. Fold into beaten egg mixture in 2 batches, and pour over base. Return pan to oven, and bake until topping is set, about 40 minutes. Remove pan to wire rack to cool completely.

◊ Using foil as a guide, remove cookie mixture from pan, and set on board. Peel off foil, and cut into bars. Dust lightly with confectioners' sugar. Store in airtight containers in single layers.

CARAMEL CASHEW-ALMOND SQUARES

LEFT & BELOW

ABOUT **3** DOZEN

This is a delicious bar cookie with a rich, sticky topping of caramelized honey and nuts. Not for calorie counters!

INGREDIENTS

PASTRY CRUST

◊ 3 cups all-purpose flour

◊ ½ cup cornstarch

◊ ½ tsp salt

◊ 1½ cups (3 sticks) unsalted butter, softened

◊ ⅔ cup sugar

◊ grated zest of 1 lemon

CARAMEL NUT TOPPING

◊ 10 tbsp (1¼ sticks) unsalted butter

◊ ½ cup packed dark brown sugar

◊ ½ cup honey

◊ 2 cups salted cashews, lightly toasted and coarsely chopped

◊ 1 cup whole blanched almonds, toasted and coarsely chopped

◊ 2½ tbsp whipping cream

◊ Prepare a 13- by 9-inch baking pan (see page 102).

◊ Into a medium bowl, sift together flour, cornstarch and salt. In a large bowl with electric mixer, beat butter, sugar and lemon zest until light and fluffy, 1 to 2 minutes. On low speed, beat in flour mixture until blended and soft dough forms. Scrape down sides of bowl, and refrigerate dough, 10 minutes.

◊ Turn dough out onto a large sheet of waxed paper, and pat into a rectangle. Cover with another piece of waxed paper, and roll out to 15- by 10-inch rectangle. Slide onto baking sheet, and refrigerate, 10 minutes.

◊ Discard top layer of waxed paper, and carefully invert pastry into foil-lined dish. Remove remaining paper, and press pastry onto bottom and 1 inch up sides of pan, pressing into corners. Prick bottom of pastry with a fork, and bake until pastry is lightly colored, about 30 minutes, turning pan halfway through cooking and pricking with fork if pastry puffs during baking. Remove pan to wire rack.

◊ In a medium saucepan over medium heat, bring butter, sugar and honey to a boil, stirring until sugar dissolves. Then boil without stirring until mixture thickens slightly, about 1 minute. Remove from heat and stir in cashews, almonds and cream until well-mixed.

◊ Pour nut mixture over crust, spreading evenly. Bake until sticky and bubbling, about 20 minutes. Remove to wire rack to cool completely. Using foil as a guide, remove cookie mixture to a board. Peel off foil, and cut into 1½-inch squares. Store in airtight containers in single layers.

MERINGUE-TOPPED BUTTERSCOTCH FINGERS

LEFT & RIGHT

ABOUT 1 DOZEN

These chewy bar cookies combine a soft, dark toffee layer and a silky meringue nut topping.

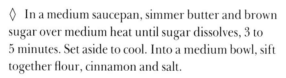

BUTTERSCOTCH LAYER

◊ ¼ cup (½ stick) unsalted butter

◊ 1 cup packed dark brown sugar

◊ 1 egg

◊ 1 tsp vanilla extract

◊ ½ cup all-purpose flour

◊ 1 tsp ground cinnamon

◊ ½ tsp salt

MERINGUE TOPPING

◊ 1 egg white

◊ ⅛ tsp cream of tartar

◊ 1 tbsp corn syrup

◊ ½ cup superfine sugar

◊ 1 cup chopped walnuts

◊ In a medium saucepan, simmer butter and brown sugar over medium heat until sugar dissolves, 3 to 5 minutes. Set aside to cool. Into a medium bowl, sift together flour, cinnamon and salt.

◊ Preheat oven to 350°F. Prepare an 8-inch square baking pan. (See page 102.)

◊ Beat egg and vanilla extract into cooled butter mixture until well-blended. Stir in flour mixture until just blended. Spread over bottom of prepared pan, smoothing top evenly.

◊ In a medium bowl, beat egg white until foamy. Add cream of tartar and continue beating until soft peaks form. Gradually beat in corn syrup, then sugar, and continue beating until whites are stiff and glossy. Fold in half the nuts, and carefully spread topping over butterscotch layer. Sprinkle top with remaining nuts.

◊ Bake until topping is puffed (meringue may crack) and golden, about 30 minutes. Remove to wire rack and cool completely. Using foil as a guide, remove cookie mixture to a board and peel off foil. Cut into fingers.

FLAPJACKS

NOT ILLUSTRATED

ABOUT 8 TO 16

This is an easy-to-make, old-fashioned cookie made from dark brown sugar or molasses and oats – sweet and chewy.

INGREDIENTS

◊ ¼ cup (½ stick) butter

◊ 1½ tbsp dark corn syrup

◊ ⅓ cup packed dark brown sugar

◊ 1¼ cup old-fashioned oats

◊ ½ cup chopped walnuts, pecans or hazelnuts

◊ ¼ tsp salt

◊ Preheat oven to 350°F. Line an 8-inch cake pan with non-stick baking parchment or foil. Lightly oil parchment or foil.

◊ In a medium saucepan, cook butter, syrup and sugar over medium heat until melted and well-blended, 2 to 3 minutes. Remove from the heat, and stir in oats, chopped nuts and salt until blended. Pour into prepared pan, and smooth top.

◊ Bake until crisp and golden brown, 20 to 25 minutes. Remove pan to wire rack to cool slightly, 5 to 10 minutes. Invert onto a board, peel off paper, and, while still warm, cut into 8 or 16 equal wedges. Return to wire rack to cool completely. Store in airtight containers.

LEMON CHEESECAKE FINGERS

ABOVE & BELOW

ABOUT 1 DOZEN

INGREDIENTS

PECAN CRUST

◊ 1 cup all-purpose flour

◊ ½ cup pecans, finely chopped

◊ ⅓ cup packed light brown sugar

◊ 6 tbsp (¾ stick) unsalted butter, softened

CHEESECAKE TOPPING

◊ 8 oz cream cheese, softened

◊ ¼ cup sugar

◊ 1 tbsp sour cream

◊ grated zest of 1 lemon

◊ 1 tbsp lemon juice

◊ 1 tsp vanilla extract

◊ 1 egg

◊ ½ cup pecans, finely chopped

◊ confectioners' sugar for dusting and grated lemon zest for decorating

◊ Preheat oven to 350°F. Prepare a 9-inch square baking pan (see page 102).

◊ In a medium bowl, stir together flour, chopped pecans and sugar. Using pastry blender or fingertips, cut in butter until crumbs form. Press evenly into bottom of foil-lined pan. Bake until golden, 12 to 15 minutes. Remove pan to wire rack.

◊ In a medium bowl with electric mixer, beat softened cream cheese and sugar until light and fluffy, 1 to 2 minutes. Beat in sour cream, lemon zest and juice, vanilla extract and egg until well-blended. Pour over baked crust, and sprinkle with the chopped pecans.

◊ Bake until puffed and golden, about 25 minutes. Remove to wire rack to cool completely; then refrigerate until well chilled, 2 to 3 hours. Using foil as a guide, remove cheesecake to a board. Peel off foil, and, using a sharp knife, cut into 24 bars.

> **TIP**
> For orange-flavor bars, use 1 tablespoon orange zest and 1 tablespoon orange juice instead of lemon.

PECAN-SESAME FINGERS

ABOUT 3 DOZEN

The toasted sesame seeds provide an unusual flavor to this chewy bar cookie.

INGREDIENTS

SESAME CRUST

◊ ½ cup (1 stick) unsalted butter, softened

◊ ½ cup packed brown sugar

◊ 1 tsp sesame oil (optional)

◊ 1 cup all-purpose flour

◊ ½ cup sesame seeds, toasted

PECAN TOPPING

◊ 2 eggs

◊ 1 cup packed brown sugar

◊ 1 tsp vanilla extract

◊ 2 tbsp all-purpose flour

◊ 1 tsp baking powder

◊ ½ tsp salt

◊ 1½ cups chopped pecans

◊ 1¼ cups sweetened flaked coconut

◊ 2-3 tbsp sesame seeds for sprinkling

◊ Preheat oven to 375°F. Well grease a 13- by 9-inch baking pan. In a large bowl, with electric mixer, beat butter, sugar and sesame oil, if using, until light and fluffy, 1 to 2 minutes. Beat in flour and sesame seeds until soft dough forms. Push dough evenly onto bottom of prepared pan, smoothing top. Bake 10 minutes.

◊ Meanwhile prepare topping. In a large bowl with electric beater, beat eggs, brown sugar, vanilla extract, flour, baking powder and salt until light and fluffy, 1 to 2 minutes. Fold in pecans and coconut.

◊ Remove crust to wire rack. Pour over egg-pecan mixture, and sprinkle with sesame seeds. Bake until top is firm and golden, 15 to 20 minutes. Remove baking pan to wire rack, and cool completely.

◊ Run a sharp knife around sides of pan to loosen mixture, and carefully slide onto a board. Cut into 1½-inch bars.

> **TIP**
> If bar is difficult to remove from baking pan, cut into bars or squares, and store in baking pan covered with plastic wrap or foil.

CHOCOLATE PEANUT BUTTER BARS

ABOUT 2 DOZEN

This most popular combination of chocolate and peanut butter is wonderful as a glazed brownie filled with chocolate chips and peanuts.

INGREDIENTS

◊ 1 cup smooth or chunky peanut butter, softened

◊ 6 tbsp (¾ stick) butter, softened

◊ 1 cup sugar

◊ 3 eggs

◊ 1 tsp vanilla extract

◊ 1 cup all-purpose flour

◊ 1 cup semisweet chocolate chips

◊ 1 cup salted peanuts, chopped

GLAZE

◊ 6 oz semisweet chocolate, chopped

◊ 2 tbsp smooth peanut butter

◊ 2 tbsp butter

◊ 2 tbsp corn syrup

◊ 1 tsp vanilla extract

◊ Preheat oven to 350°F. Prepare a 13- by 9-inch baking pan (see page 102).

◊ In a large bowl, beat peanut butter and butter until creamy and smooth, 30 to 60 seconds. Add sugar, eggs and vanilla extract. Stir in flour until blended; then stir in chocolate chips and peanuts. Spread batter into prepared pan, smoothing top.

◊ Bake until golden round the edges, 25 to 30 minutes. Remove pan to wire rack to cool completely.

◊ In a medium saucepan over low heat, melt chocolate, peanut butter, butter, corn syrup and vanilla until smooth, stirring frequently. Remove from heat, and cool until slightly thickened, stirring occasionally.

◊ Using foil as a guide, remove brownies from pan, and invert onto a board or baking sheet. Using a metal palette knife, spread glaze over brownie. Refrigerate until set, about 1 hour.

◊ Using a long-bladed, sharp knife, cut into 48 1½-inch bars. Store in airtight containers in single layers, or refrigerate in an airtight container with waxed paper between layers.

CHOCOLATE CHIP PECAN SHORTBREAD

LEFT & RIGHT

32 PIECES

This is a rich shortbread speckled with chocolate chips and finely ground pecans. It is one of my favorite cookies and is so easy to make.

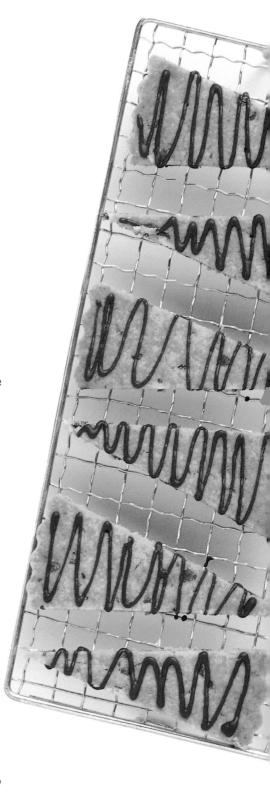

INGREDIENTS

◊ 1 cup pecans, toasted and cooled

◊ 1¾ cups all-purpose flour

◊ ¼ cup cornstarch

◊ ½ cup confectioners' sugar

◊ ¼ tsp salt

◊ 1 cup (2 sticks) unsalted butter, softened

◊ 1 cup mini semisweet chocolate chips

◊ 1½ oz semisweet chocolate melted for drizzling

TIP

*T*o remove side from pan with a removable bottom, set pan on a large can (such as tomatoes), and allow side to drop to work surface, thus releasing bottom with pie, or, in this case, shortbread. This avoids breaking the delicate edges.

◊ Preheat oven to 325°F. Lightly grease two 8-inch pie pans with removable bottoms. In a food processor fitted with metal blade, process toasted pecans until very fine crumbs form; do not overprocess or nuts may form a paste and release oil. Pour into a large bowl.

◊ Into ground nuts, sift together flour, cornstarch, confectioners' sugar and salt, and mix well. Add butter and, using a pastry blender or fingertips, blend well until dough holds together. Stir in chocolate chips.

◊ Divide dough evenly between the pie pans, and pat onto bottom in an even layer. Bake until edges are golden and surface appears slightly puffed, 20 to 25 minutes. Remove pans to wire racks to cool, about 5 minutes.

◊ Carefully remove side of each pan, and place pan bottom with shortbread on heat-proof surface. Cut each shortbread circle into 16 thin wedges; this must be done while shortbread is warm and soft, or it will break. Return shortbread wedges on their bases to wire racks to cool completely.

◊ Using a metal palette knife, remove shortbread wedges to wire rack, arranging top-to-toe to fit the wedges close together on rack. Spoon melted chocolate into paper cone (page 14), and drizzle wedges evenly. Store in airtight containers with waxed paper between layers.

113

7

SPECIAL Cookies

These are slightly more complicated cookies.

They are usually based on one of the previous

methods, but each one has a special feature.

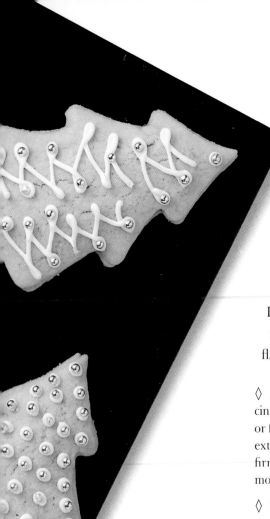

MINCEMEAT CHRISTMAS-TREE COOKIES

LEFT & RIGHT

ABOUT 3 DOZEN

Individual mince pies are traditional Christmas treats in Great Britain. The same textures and flavors are used in these festive, seasonal cookies.

◊ In a large bowl, sift together flours, baking powder, cinnamon or mixed spice and salt. With pastry blender or fingertips, mix in butter, shortening, eggs, vanilla extract and 1 to 2 tablespoons brandy or water, until a firm dough forms. If dough is too dry, sprinkle in a little more brandy or water.

◊ Scrape dough out onto piece of plastic wrap or waxed paper and, using wrap or paper as a guide, shape dough into a flat disk. Refrigerate until firm, 2 to 3 hours.

◊ Preheat oven to 400°F. Lightly grease 2 large baking sheets. On a lightly floured surface, using floured rolling pin, roll out half the dough $1/16$ inch thick (keep remaining dough refrigerated). With a floured 3-inch Christmas tree or other cutter, cut as many shapes as possible; you will need an even number to sandwich.

◊ Place a tablespoon of mincemeat on half the cookies, spreading to within $1/4$ inch of the edge. Top with another cookie, lightly pressing edges together. Place cookies 1 inch apart on baking sheets. Bake until golden, 10 to 15 minutes. Remove baking sheets from oven to cool slightly. Then, using a metal pancake turner, remove cookies to wire racks to cool completely. Repeat with remaining dough and trimmings, and mincemeat.

◊ Into a small bowl, sift confectioners' sugar and cream of tartar. With an electric mixer, beat in egg white and vanilla extract until very stiff and a knife drawn through mixture leaves a clean path. If mixture is too thin, beat in a little more sugar. If too thick, add a few drops of water. Cover bowl with plastic wrap to prevent surface from crusting. Spoon icing into a paper cone (page 14), and use to pipe decorations onto cookie trees, adding a few silver dragées as Christmas balls. Allow icing to set until firm, 1 to 2 hours.

INGREDIENTS

◊ 2 cups all-purpose flour

◊ ½ cup whole wheat flour

◊ 1 tsp baking powder

◊ ½ tsp ground cinnamon or mixed spice

◊ ½ tsp salt

◊ ¼ cup (½ stick) unsalted butter, softened

◊ ¼ cup white vegetable shortening, softened

◊ 2 eggs

◊ 1 tsp vanilla extract

◊ 2 to 3 tbsp brandy or water

◊ 2 to 2½ cups mincemeat

ROYAL ICING

◊ 1¼ cups confectioners' sugar

◊ ¼ tsp cream of tartar

◊ 1 egg white

◊ ½ tsp vanilla extract

◊ silver dragées for decoration

TIP
Silver dragées (pronounced drah-zjays) are available in some large supermarkets or specialty cookware shops.

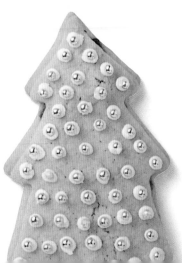

116

LADYFINGERS

NOT ILLUSTRATED

ABOUT 3 DOZEN

This classic French "cookie" is often used to line molds for custard-based desserts, but is wonderful on its own. In France these elegant, tender cookies accompany champagne!

INGREDIENTS

◊ ¾ cup all-purpose flour, sifted twice

◊ 4 eggs, separated

◊ ¾ cup superfine sugar

◊ 1 tsp vanilla extract

◊ ⅛ tsp cream of tartar

◊ confectioners' sugar for dusting

◊ Preheat oven to 350°F. Lightly grease and flour 2 large baking sheets. In a medium bowl with electric mixer, beat egg yolks, ½ cup of the sugar and the vanilla extract until very thick and pale and mixture leaves a ribbon trail when lifted from bowl, 5 to 7 minutes. Gently stir in flour until just blended.

◊ In a large bowl with cleaned beaters, beat egg whites and cream of tartar on low speed until foamy. Increase speed and continue beating until stiff peaks form. Sprinkle in remaining sugar, a tablespoon at a time, beating well after each addition until stiff and glossy. Fold a third of whites into yolk mixture; then, in 3 batches, fold yolk mixture into remaining whites.

◊ Gently spoon batter into a large pastry bag fitted with a ½-inch plain tip. Pipe batter in 3½-inch lengths, 1½ inches apart, onto prepared baking sheets. Dust cookies generously with confectioners' sugar.

◊ Bake until golden, about 15 minutes. Remove baking sheets to wire racks to cool, 5 to 7 minutes. Then remove ladyfingers to wire racks to cool completely.

TIP

*T*o fill a large (15-inch) pastry bag with liquidy mixture such as above, drop in the tip and secure. Fold down a 2-inch cuff on the outside of the bag. Twist the tube end of the bag and push it into the tip. This prevents any batter leaking out. Place the bag in a tall measuring cup to hold it upright and steady while you fill it.

CHOCOLATE-DIPPED PALMIERS

ABOVE & BELOW

ABOUT 40

INGREDIENTS

◊ ½ cup finely chopped hazelnuts

◊ 2 tbsp sugar

◊ ½ tsp ground cinnamon

◊ sugar for rolling

◊ 8 oz fresh or frozen puff pastry, defrosted if frozen

1 egg, lightly beaten

◊ 8 oz semisweet chocolate

◊ Lightly grease 2 large baking sheets. In a small bowl, combine hazelnuts, sugar and cinnamon. Set aside.

◊ Cut pastry into quarters. Generously sprinkle work-surface with sugar and roll out one quarter of pastry to a thin rectangle. Lightly brush pastry with beaten egg, and sprinkle evenly with the nut mixture.

◊ Fold long edges of pastry inward to meet, edge to edge, in center. Brush surface with a little more beaten egg, and sprinkle with more nut mixture. Then fold outside edges inward to meet, edge to edge, in center to make 4 even layers.

◊ Preheat oven to 425°F. Using a sharp knife, cut pastry crosswise into 1-inch strips, and place ½ inch apart on baking sheets. Open from center fold to form a "V" shape. Refrigerate 15 minutes.

◊ Bake until golden, about 10 minutes, turning palmiers over halfway through cooking time. Remove baking sheets to wire racks to cool slightly. Then remove palmiers to wire racks to cool completely.

◊ In a small heat-proof bowl set over a saucepan of just simmering water, melt the chocolate until smooth, stirring frequently. Line baking sheets with waxed paper or foil. Dip each palmier halfway into chocolate and place on lined baking sheets. Allow to set.

PECAN TASSIES

ABOVE & BELOW

ABOUT 2 DOZEN

These American cookies from the Southern pecan-growing regions taste as delicious as they sound. Considered a "cookie," it is really a mini tartlet of tender, cream-cheese pastry filled with a caramelized pecan center.

INGREDIENTS

CREAM-CHEESE PASTRY

◊ 1 cup all-purpose flour

◊ 1 tbsp sugar

◊ ¼ tsp salt

◊ ¼ tsp ground nutmeg

◊ ½ cup (1 stick) unsalted butter, softened

◊ 4 oz cream cheese, softened

PECAN FILLING

◊ 1 egg

◊ ½ cup packed dark brown sugar

◊ 1 tsp vanilla extract

◊ 1½ tbsp unsalted butter, melted

◊ ½ cup pecans, toasted and chopped

◊ 24 pecan halves for decoration

◊ Lightly butter 2 12-cup or 1 24-cup muffin pans. Into a medium bowl, sift together flour, sugar, salt and nutmeg. Add butter and cream cheese, and, using a pastry blender or fingertips, cut in butter until blended and soft dough forms. Cover bowl, and refrigerate until just firm enough to roll, about 10 minutes.

◊ On a lightly floured surface, using a floured rolling pin, roll out dough ⅜ inch thick. Using a floured 2½-inch fluted cutter, cut out 24 rounds. Carefully line each muffin pan cup with a pastry round, gently pressing pastry onto bottom and side of cups. Refrigerate 20 to 30 minutes. (If using a 12-cup muffin cup pan, refrigerate remaining rounds until first batch is baked.)

◊ In a medium bowl with electric mixer, beat eggs until foamy. Gradually beat in brown sugar, vanilla and melted butter. Sprinkle an equal amount of chopped pecans into each cup. Carefully ladle some filling into each muffin cup, and top with a pecan half.

◊ Bake tassies until tops are puffed and filling set (pastry edges will be golden), about 20 minutes. Remove to wire rack to cool, about 20 to 30 minutes. Using the top of a sharp knife, gently loosen edge of pastry from each muffin cup and unmold each cookie. Serve warm or cool completely, then store in airtight containers.

> **TIP**
>
> *F*illing can be made with toasted chopped walnuts, hazelnuts, macadamias or even, and especially, pine nuts, but pecans are traditional.

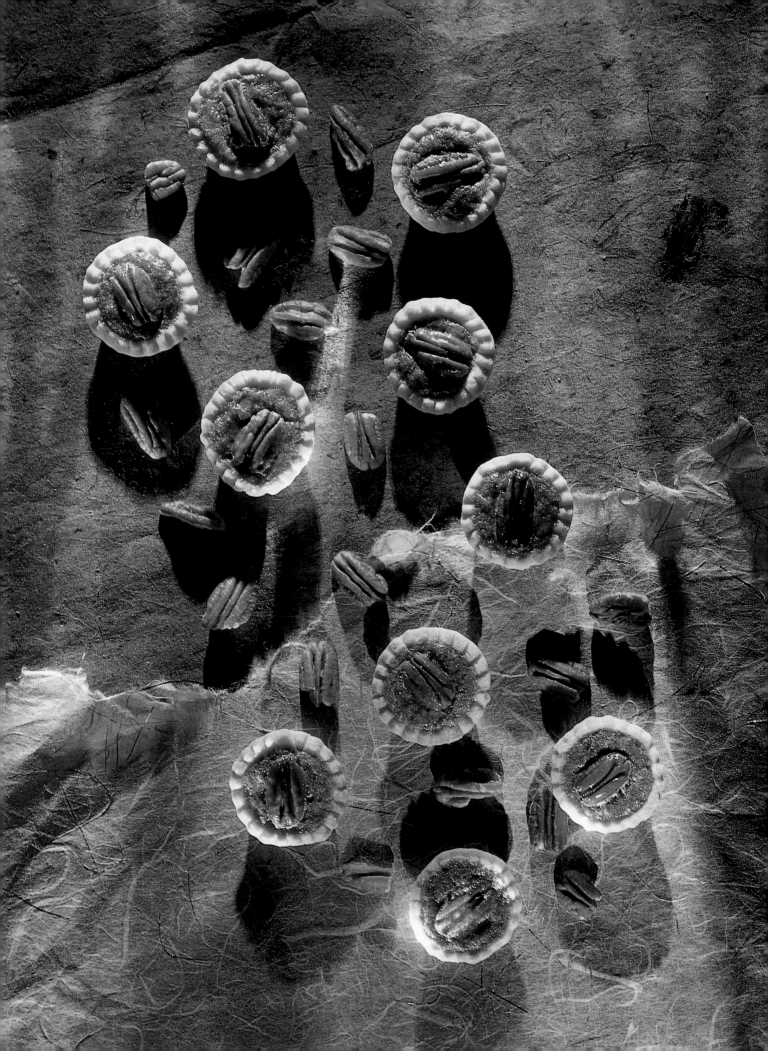

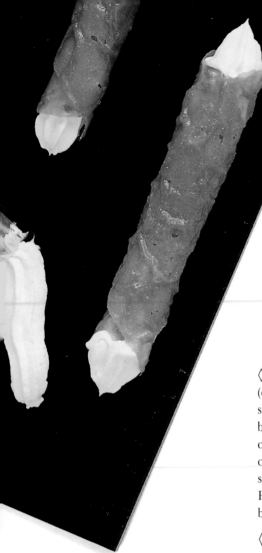

CREAM-FILLED BRANDY SNAPS

LEFT & BELOW

ABOUT 2½ DOZEN

These lacy, brandy-scented cookies are sometimes called English Rolled Wafers. Filled with a brandied, whipped cream they are the most elegant of tea-time treats.

◊ Preheat oven to 350°F. Butter 2 large baking sheets (or more if you have them), or use non-stick baking sheets. Lightly oil 2 wooden spoon handles. In a heavy-bottomed saucepan over medium heat, bring butter, corn syrup, sugars and ginger to a boil, stirring constantly until sugars dissolve. Remove from heat, and stir in brandy and flour until well-blended and smooth. Place pan in a shallow bowl of hot water (this will keep batter from hardening while shaping cookies).

◊ Begin by working in batches of 4 cookies on each sheet. Drop tablespoonfuls of batter about 6 inches apart on baking sheet. Using the back of a moistened spoon, spread each mound into about 3-inch rounds (cookies will spread further). Bake until golden and bubbling, 7 to 10 minutes, turning baking sheet if cookies color unevenly.

◊ Remove baking sheet to wire rack and cool, about 1 minute. Working quickly, use a thin-bladed, metal palette knife to loosen the edge of a hot cookie and lift it off. Roll cookie around the oiled handle of a wooden spoon, pressing down on seam for a few seconds. Repeat with another cookie.

◊ Slide off handle, and place on wire rack to cool completely. If cookies become too brittle to roll, return baking sheet to the oven for 30 seconds to soften. (Cookies should be flexible but firm enough to lift off without wrinkling and tearing.)

◊ Up to 2 hours before serving, in a large bowl with electric mixer, beat cream, vanilla extract and brandy until stiff peaks form. Spoon cream into a medium pastry bag fitted with a medium star tip. Pipe cream into both ends of each brandy snap cookie and place on a baking sheet. Refrigerate until ready to serve (do not fill too early or moisture will soften brandy snaps).

VARIATION

*F*or lemon cream filling, omit brandy and vanilla extract. Whip cream with ½ teaspoon lemon extract, and beat in about 1 cup lemon curd, bought or use lemon curd filling from Lemon Cookie Tarts (opposite).

TIP

*B*randy snap batter can be made into "tulip cups" for ice cream or fruit salads. Follow shaping procedure for Tulipes (page 121).

INGREDIENTS

COOKIES

◊ ½ cup (1 stick) unsalted butter, cut into pieces

◊ 3 tbsp corn syrup

◊ ¼ cup sugar

◊ ¼ cup packed light brown sugar

◊ 1 tsp ground ginger

◊ 2 tbsp brandy

◊ ½ cup all-purpose flour

BRANDY CREAM

◊ 1¼ cups whipping cream

◊ ½ tsp vanilla extract

◊ 2 tbsp brandy

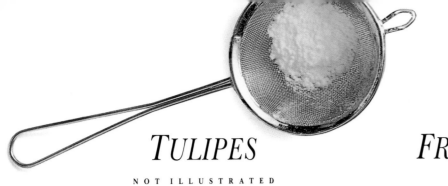

TULIPES

NOT ILLUSTRATED

ABOUT 1 DOZEN

These elegant little tulip-shaped cups make a spectacular dessert filled with ice cream, sorbets or cut-up fruits. Like the Almond Tile Cookies (page 127) they take a little patience and practice.

INGREDIENTS

◊ 2 egg whites

◊ ½ tsp vanilla extract or ¼ tsp lemon extract

◊ 1 tsp grated lemon zest

◊ ½ cup all-purpose flour, sifted

◊ ½ cup superfine sugar

◊ ¼ tsp salt

◊ Preheat oven to 400°F. Generously butter 2 baking sheets. In a medium bowl with electric mixer, beat egg whites until foamy. Add vanilla or lemon extract, lemon zest, flour and salt, and beat until smooth and well-blended.

◊ Begin by working in batches of 2 cookies on each sheet. Drop a tablespoon of batter in diagonal corners of a baking sheet, and, using back of a spoon, spread evenly into 4-inch rounds; they do not have to be perfect.

◊ Bake until edges are golden and centers are set but still pale 4–5 minutes. Remove baking sheet to wire rack, and, working quickly, use a thin-bladed metal palette knife to loosen the edge of a hot cookie. Lift cookie off baking sheet and invert centered over an upturned custard cup, small glass or ramekin. Using your hands, gently press cookie down to shape tulip. Alternatively, use another cup or glass pressed upside down over the hot cookie to shape the tulip.

◊ Repeat with the second cookie as quickly as possible. Remove cookies from mold, and transfer to wire racks to cool completely. Repeat with remaining batter, cooling and regreasing baking sheets if necessary. Store in airtight containers in single layers.

> **TIP**
> To recrisp cookies if necessary, see Almond Tile Cookies (page 127).

FRIED BOW TIES

ABOVE

ABOUT 6 DOZEN

Fried cookies are traditional in many countries such as Mexico, Italy, Spain and the Middle East. These are so pretty and just as easy.

INGREDIENTS

◊ 3 eggs

◊ ¼ cup milk

◊ ¼ cup sugar

◊ ½ tsp salt

◊ 2¾ cups all-purpose flour

◊ vegetable oil for frying

◊ confectioners' sugar for dusting

◊ In a large bowl with electric mixer, beat eggs, milk, sugar and salt until blended. On low speed, beat in 1½ cups of the flour, then stir in remaining flour to form a soft dough. Scrape dough onto a sheet of plastic wrap or waxed paper; flatten to a disk shape. Refrigerate until firm, 2 to 3 hours.

◊ On a lightly floured surface, using a floured rolling pin, roll out half the dough as thin as possible, ⅛ inch thick or thinner. Cut dough into 4- by 1½-inch rectangles. Using a sharp knife, cut a 1-inch lengthwise slit in center of each strip; carefully pull one end of rectangle through center slit to form the bow-tie shape. Repeat with remaining dough.

◊ In a deep-fat fryer or deep-sided, heavy skillet, heat about 1 inch oil to 350°F on a deep-fat thermometer. Carefully drop in a few bow ties at a time, and fry until golden, about 1½ minutes. With a slotted metal pancake turner or spoon, remove to double thickness of paper towels to drain; cool completely. Dust with confectioners' sugar. These cookies are best eaten on the same day.

> **TIP**
> If you do not have a deep-fat thermometer, test oil temperature by dropping a ¼-inch cube of bread into hot oil. It should fry to golden-brown in 30 to 40 seconds.

LEMON COOKIE TARTS

ABOUT 3 DOZEN

These are little tart shells made from a sweet cookie dough. The lemon curd is particularly delicious, but raspberry or apricot preserves could be used instead.

INGREDIENTS

COOKIE DOUGH

◊ ½ cup (1 stick) unsalted butter, softened

◊ ½ cup superfine sugar

◊ 1 egg yolk

◊ ½ tsp almond extract

◊ 1¾ cups all-purpose flour

LEMON CURD

◊ ¾ cup sugar

◊ ⅓ cup water

◊ ¼ cup all-purpose flour

◊ grated zest and juice of 1 lemon

◊ ⅛ tsp salt

◊ 2 eggs, lightly beaten

◊ lemon zest to decorate, optional

◊ In a large bowl, beat the butter until creamy, 30 seconds. Add sugar and beat until light and fluffy, 1 to 2 minutes. Beat in egg yolk and almond extract. On low speed, beat in flour until soft dough forms. Scrape down side of bowl. Refrigerate, covered, until firm.

◊ Preheat oven to 350°F. Use a teaspoon to scoop out dough and form into 36 ¾-inch balls. Press a ball of dough into bottom and up side of tiny fluted tart or brioche molds. Prick bottom and side of dough to prevent puffing. Place molds on baking sheet and bake until just golden, 15 to 20 minutes. Remove molds to wire racks to cool, 10 minutes; then carefully remove cookie-tart shells from molds to cool on wire racks.

◊ Prepare lemon curd. In a medium saucepan, whisk together sugar, water, flour, lemon zest and juice, salt and eggs. Over medium-low heat, cook until thickened, 8 to 10 minutes. Pour into chilled bowl and cool, stirring occasionally to prevent skin forming. Refrigerate until very cold and thickened.

◊ About 1 hour before serving, spoon a little lemon curd into cookie tart. Unfilled cookies can be stored in airtight containers with waxed paper between layers.

COCONUT FORTUNE COOKIES

ABOUT 3 DOZEN

Everyone knows these Chinese cookies – this one has a pretty texture provided by a little grated coconut.

INGREDIENTS

◊ 2 egg whites

◊ ⅓ cup confectioners' sugar, sifted

◊ 1 tsp coconut or almond extract

◊ 2 tbsp unsalted butter, melted

◊ ⅓ cup cake flour, sifted

◊ ¼ cup sweetened shredded coconut, toasted and chopped

◊ Grease and flour 2 baking sheets. Using a glass 3 inches in diameter, mark two circles in diagonal corners of each baking sheet (cookies will spread).

◊ In a medium bowl with electric mixer, beat egg whites until foamy. Gradually beat in confectioners' sugar, coconut or almond extract and melted butter. On low speed, beat in flour until well-blended.

◊ Drop a level teaspoonful of batter in centers of each marked circle on baking sheets. Using the back of a spoon, spread evenly to cover circles completely. Sprinkle each cookie with a little toasted coconut.

◊ Bake, one sheet at a time, until edges are lightly browned, about 5 minutes. Remove baking sheet to wire rack and working quickly, use a thin-bladed, metal palette knife to loosen edge of a cookie. Set on a board, fold in half and then curve each cookie over the rim of a glass creating the classic shape; hold for 30 seconds. Place on a wire rack to cool.

◊ Repeat with remaining cookies. If cookies become too crisp to remove and shape, return to oven for 30 seconds to soften.

> **TIP**
> Coconut extract can be found in specialty food stores and some health food stores, but almond extract will also give a lovely flavor.

PIZZELLES

LEFT

ABOUT 4 DOZEN

These Italian cookies are really like little waffles.
Use any shape waffle iron you like, but heart shape
is prettiest.

INGREDIENTS

◊ 1¾ cups all-purpose flour

◊ 2 tsp baking powder

◊ ½ tsp salt

◊ 3 eggs, lightly beaten

◊ ¾ cup sugar

◊ ½ cup unsalted butter, melted

◊ 2 tbsp anise flavor or vanilla extract

◊ confectioners' sugar for dusting

◊ Preheat a 7-inch electric pizzelle or other waffle iron
as manufacturer directs. Into a large bowl, sift together
the flour, baking powder and salt.

◊ Make well in center of flour mixture, and pour in
eggs, sugar, melted butter and anise flavor or vanilla
extract. With electric mixer on low speed, beat liquid
ingredients until blended, then slowly incorporate flour
from edge of well until it is all blended and mixture is
smooth. (If batter is too thick, thin with a little milk or
water.)

◊ Using a small ladle, pour about 2 tablespoons of
batter into center of pizzelle iron. Pull down cover and
allow to bake, without lifting cover, for manufacturers'
specified time.

◊ Lift cover, and use a metal palette knife or fork to lift
edge of pizzelle. Slide onto wire rack to cool completely.
Repeat with remaining batter. Dust pizzelles with
confectioners' sugar. Store in airtight containers.
Alternatively, keep pizzelles warm in a 250°F oven, and
serve dusted with confectioners' sugar and with a little
preserve or maple syrup.

> **TIP**
> *P*izzelle irons and waffle irons are available in
> electric and non-electric models and in
> different shapes and sizes. Be sure to follow
> each manufacturers' instructions for use
> and cooking times.

APRICOT-CHOCOLATE CHIP RUGELACH

RIGHT & BELOW

ABOUT 5 ½ DOZEN

Rugelach are traditional Jewish cookies, made with flaky cream cheese pastry. They are traditionally filled with poppy seed paste.

INGREDIENTS

◊ 2 cups all-purpose flour

◊ ½ tsp salt

◊ ½ cup (1 stick) unsalted butter, softened

◊ 4 oz cream cheese, softened

◊ ¼ cup sour cream

◊ 3 tbsp superfine sugar

◊ 1 egg, separated

◊ 1 cup apricot preserves

◊ ½ cup mini-semisweet chocolate chips or 3 oz chopped, semisweet chocolate

◊ ¼ cup flaked almonds

◊ ¼ cup superfine sugar

◊ Into a large bowl, sift flour and salt. Add butter, cream cheese, sour cream, sugar and egg yolk. Using a pastry blender or fingertips, knead mixture until soft dough forms and holds together. Shape dough into a ball and flatten to a disk; wrap tightly and refrigerate until firm enough to handle, 1 to 2 hours.

◊ Preheat oven to 350°F. Lightly grease 2 large baking sheets. On a lightly floured surface, using a floured rolling pin, roll out one-quarter of the dough ⅛ inch thick (keep remaining dough refrigerated). Using a plate as a guide, cut dough into a 10- to 11-inch round. Spread round with about 3 tablespoons apricot preserves to within ½ inch of the edge. Sprinkle with a few chocolate chips or chopped chocolate.

◊ Cut dough round into 12 or 16 equal wedges. Starting at curved edge, roll up each wedge jelly-roll fashion. Place cookies, point side down, 1½ inches apart on one prepared baking sheet. In a small bowl, beat egg white with 1 tablespoon water, and brush each cookie with a little mixture. Sprinkle each cookie with a few flaked almonds and a little sugar.

◊ Bake until puffed and golden brown, 20 to 25 minutes, rotating baking sheet from front to back halfway through. Remove baking sheet to wire rack to cool slightly. Then remove cookies to wire rack to cool completely.

LEMON-GINGER FLORENTINES

LEFT & RIGHT

ABOUT 30

Although these florentines are usually coated in dark chocolate, white chocolate can also be used, but it must be melted with great care. Alternatively, dip half the cookie in melted dark or white chocolate for a different effect.

INGREDIENTS

◊ ½ cup heavy cream

◊ ¼ cup (½ stick) butter

◊ ½ cup superfine sugar

◊ 2 tbsp honey

◊ 1⅔ cups slivered almonds

◊ 5 tbsp all-purpose flour

◊ grated zest of ½ lemon

◊ ¾ tsp ground ginger

◊ ½ cup dried stem or crystallized ginger

◊ ½ cup diced candied citron (lemon peel)

◊ ½ cup mini chocolate chips (optional)

◊ 8 oz semisweet chocolate, melted

◊ Preheat oven to 350°F. Lightly grease 2 large *non-stick* baking sheets. In a medium saucepan over low heat, stir cream, butter, sugar and honey until sugar is dissolved. Increase heat to high, and bring mixture to a boil, stirring constantly. Remove from heat, and stir in almonds, flour, lemon zest and ground ginger until well-blended; then stir in diced ginger and citron.

◊ Drop teaspoonfuls, at least 3 inches apart, onto prepared baking sheets. Moisten back of a spoon, and spread each circle as thin as possible. If using, sprinkle each cookie with a few chocolate chips.

◊ Bake 8 to 10 minutes, until edges are golden and cookies are bubbling. Do not overbake as the cookies can burn easily; but equally do not underbake, or cookies will be too sticky to handle. Remove baking sheets to wire racks to cool slightly. For perfectly round cookies, use a 3- or 4-inch round cookie cutter to help round edges while cookies are still hot on baking sheet. Cool until just set; then, using a thin, metal palette knife, carefully remove cookies to wire racks to cool completely.

◊ When completely cooled, spread melted chocolate on flat side of each cookie, and place chocolate side-up on wire racks. Refrigerate until chocolate is just setting, 2 to 3 minutes. If you like, spread each cookie with the chocolate and using a serrated knife or 4-tined fork, make wavy lines on chocolate layer. Alternatively, dip half the cookie in the chocolate, and place on wire racks to set. Refrigerate to set completely, 10 to 15 minutes. Store in refrigerator in airtight containers with waxed paper between layers.

SPRINGERLE

NOT ILLUSTRATED

ABOUT 6 DOZEN

These cookies, German in origin, are made with a special springerle mold or rolling pin that embosses the dough with a variety of designs.

INGREDIENTS

◊ 4 eggs
◊ 2 cups sugar
◊ 1½ tsp anise flavor
◊ 4 to 4½ cups all-purpose flour
◊ food coloring for painting (optional)
◊ vodka or water
◊ anise seeds for sprinkling

◊ In a large bowl with electric mixer, beat eggs until very light, 2 to 3 minutes. Gradually add sugar and continue beating until very thick and creamy. On low speed, beat in anise flavor and 4 cups of the flour, until a firm dough forms; you may need to add more flour.

◊ Scrape dough onto a piece of plastic wrap or waxed paper, and, using wrap or paper, form into a flat disk shape. Wrap tightly and refrigerate about 1 hour; any longer and dough might be too firm to roll.

◊ On a lightly floured surface, using a floured rolling pin, roll out half the dough into a rectangle about ¼ inch thick (the width of the rectangle should be the same width as the springerle rolling pin). Lightly flour the springerle rolling pin, and tap off any excess flour. Roll firmly over dough to obtain clear imprint.

◊ Using a sharp knife, cut dough between each pattern, and place cookies ½ inch apart on 2 large non-stick baking sheets. Allow cookies to sit at room temperature, uncovered, overnight to dry out.

◊ Preheat oven to 300°F. Bake until cookies are very slightly colored, 25 to 30 minutes. Rotate baking sheets from top to bottom and from front to back halfway through. Cookies should be cooked through but not overbaked. Remove baking sheets to wire rack to cool slightly. Then remove cookies to wire racks to cool.

◊ To decorate, dilute food colors slightly with a little vodka or water, and use a small brush to apply the color to the raised design. Allow to dry completely before storing in airtight containers sprinkled with a few anise seeds, to "ripen" for 1 to 2 weeks.

ALMOND TILE COOKIES

ABOVE & RIGHT

ABOUT 2 ½ DOZEN

These are one of the most popular French cookies – *tuiles aux amandes* – so called because they resemble the curved roof tiles seen all over France.

INGREDIENTS

◊ ½ cup whole blanched almonds, lightly toasted
◊ ½ cup superfine sugar
◊ 3 tbsp unsalted butter, softened
◊ 2 egg whites
◊ ½ tsp almond extract
◊ ¼ cup cake flour, sifted
◊ ¾ cup flaked almonds

◊ In a food processor fitted with metal blade, process toasted almonds with 2 tablespoons of the sugar until fine crumbs form. Pour into a small bowl; set aside.

◊ Preheat oven to 400°F. Generously butter 2 baking sheets. In a medium bowl with electric mixer, beat butter until creamy, 30 seconds. Add remaining sugar, and beat until light and fluffy, 1 minute. Gradually beat in egg whites and almond extract until well-blended. Sift over already sifted flour, and fold into butter mixture; then fold in reserved almond-sugar mixture.

◊ Begin by working in batches of 4 cookies on each sheet. Drop tablespoonfuls of batter about 6 inches apart on baking sheet. With the back of a moistened spoon, spread each mound of batter into very thin 3-inch rounds. Each round should be transparent. If you make a few holes, the batter will spread and fill them in. Sprinkle tops with some flaked almonds.

◊ Bake, one sheet at a time, until edges are browned and centers just golden, 4 to 5 minutes. Remove baking sheet to wire rack and, working quickly, use a thin-bladed metal palette knife to loosen the edge of a hot cookie and transfer to a rolling pin or glass tumbler. Gently press sides down to shape each cookie.

◊ If cookies become too firm to transfer, return baking sheet to oven for 30 seconds to soften, then proceed as above. When cool, transfer immediately to airtight containers in single layers. These cookies are fragile.

INDEX